The Complete Light-Pack Camping and Trail-Foods Cookbook

The Complete Light-Pack Camping and Trail-Foods Cookbook

Edwin P. Drew

McGRAW-HILL PAPERBACKS

NEW YORK • ST. LOUIS • SAN FRANCISCO • AUCKLAND
BOGOTA • DÜSSELDORF • JOHANNESBURG • LONDON
MADRID • MEXICO • MONTREAL • NEW DELHI
PANAMA • PARIS • SÃO PAULO • SINGAPORE
SYDNEY • TOKYO • TORONTO

23456789 FGRFGR 79832109

Library of Congress Cataloging in Publication Data
Drew, Edwin P
    The complete light-pack camping and trail-food cookbook.
    Includes index.
    1. Outdoor cookery. I. Title.
TX823.D65   641.5'78   77-4717
ISBN 0-07-017843-7

Dedicated to my wife—Diane—who said:
". . . fine, if you want to write it"
and three years later could still smile.

CONTENTS

PREFACE

This book explains how to produce trail and survival foods with the lightest carrying weight, smallest bulk, greatest variety, highest food value, and best taste. Although it explains the use of virtually all types of commercially prepared trail foods (including freeze-dried and grocery items), the emphasis is on do-it-yourself preparations, such as dehydration, that often give better results; save a great deal of money and allow you to take along the foods you enjoy at home.

By preparing some foods at home, you can keep things easy afield, reducing cooking times and consuming smaller amounts of fuel—even at altitude.

Everything is simple and everything works. I've field-tested nearly all the recipes—the few I haven't tried outdoors are minor variations on established recipes.

When you finish this book you should be an excellent trail cook, whether preparing beans on a mountain or a many-course feast on a beach.

To provide easy access to information, I've tried to be as brief as completeness and clarity would allow. The book is divided into four parts. Part I covers trail equipment and cooking techniques. Part II is mostly home preparations—including purchase, preparation, and packaging of foods. Part III deals mainly with recipes and field techniques. And Part IV presents notes on nutrition, with an extensive listing of food values in relation to caloric, protein, fat, and carbohydrate content. The Appendix contains test reports on twenty different lightweight stoves.

Remember, cooking is more art than science. And good food remains good food whether it's served in a luxurious restaurant or on a bare slope.

—*Edwin P. Drew*

PART

I

TRAIL
EQUIPMENT
AND
COOKING
BASICS

HEAT SOURCES

The proper heat sources, as well as utensils, foods, and cooking methods combine to lighten your pack, shorten the time spent cooking, and increase enjoyment in the outdoors. So first let's examine what's involved.

The campfire enjoys a popularity born of tradition and of the many things it yields to body and soul. For some, camping and campfires are inseparable, and talk of eliminating the campfire—if only during cooking—is regarded as sacrilege.

Yet because of environmental concerns, campfires have been banned in many areas. And they will be subject to increasing restrictions in years to come. Aside from the campfire's ecological drawbacks, it is not an efficient heat source for cooking. It takes time to build: There's wood to gather and size, the ground to prepare, the trouble of lighting, the cultivating of embers. Then come the trials with flame, smoke, cookware, and cleanup.

For these reasons, I carry a lightweight stove. And although my discussions of trail cooking assume the presence of a cookstove, you'll find them of equal value if you cook by campfire.

There are five types of fuel used in lightweight pack stoves: kerosene, alcohol, butane, white gasoline, and solid fuel. Propane requires heavy-duty cartridges and is not included here.

STOVE ACCESSORIES

In general, wind is the most important element affecting trail stove performance. Even slight gusts cut the heat transfer. Wind leeches heat from the pot, through the sides, and from the surface of the food or water. It also blows burner heat away from the pot.

The stronger the wind and the colder the air, the more heat is leeched from the pot. Sometimes the wind (or even cold air temperature alone) negates the heat output of the stove so that the pot will never come to a boil.

A windscreen is worth its weight in fuel alone. In addition you can make your body serve as windscreen, and sitting upwind, you avoid stove fumes.

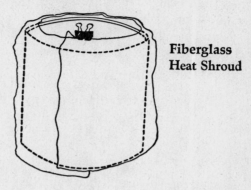

Fiberglass Heat Shroud

A pot lid will save heat in all cases. It's a must! Sometime ago I made what I call a heat shroud. It's simply a piece of fiberglass cloth 9 by 24 inches. Such cloth is available at marine supply stores and at many hardware stores. I drape the cloth over the pot, letting the cloth hang slightly lower than the pot bottom so the heat goes up the sides of the pot. I clip the ends together with a spring clip. This shroud helps hold the heat in, increasing the efficiency of the heat transfer and protecting the pot from the wind and cold.

The cloth weighs only 2 ounces and costs under a dollar.

Caution: Don't drape a shroud over a fuel tank or cartridge. An overheated tank of white gas may blow its valve, and an overheated butane cartridge might explode.

FUEL SAFETY

When using butane or white gasoline, be aware that both are extremely inflammable and both can explode. Treat them with respect and follow all of the manufacturer's instructions.

Butane cartridges must be installed and removed carefully. Here, keep them pointed away from you and companions—and away from any fire or spark. Be sure the whole stove is cool before you attempt to change butane cartridges or handle white gasoline. If you run out of fuel while cooking, wait until the unit cools.

Kerosene and alcohol are considered safe fuels—neither one will explode. But this doesn't mean you should be less cautious with them.

Never hold your head over a stove when you are lighting it. All types of units can flare during lighting.

One final caution: Never light a pack stove in a tent!

BUTANE

Butane stoves use either vaporized butane or liquid butane. With vaporized butane, the pressure in the cartridge forces the vaporized butane into the stove. With liquid-feed butane, there is a wick in the cartridge which feeds liquid butane into the stove where the butane is vaporized.

All butane stoves use a ported burner, and they all have good simmer capabilities.

At freezing temperatures and sea level, vaporized butane becomes liquid and won't vaporize until it's warmed with the hands. Liquified butane cartridges do not need the pressure and will work in temperatures below vaporized butane. Even so, butane freezes solid at 15°F.

Butane cartridges work well if cool or if as warm as your hands. There is no need to preheat them to the explosion point (around 190 to 230°F depending on altitude).

Butane stoves are most efficient with a full tank. As the tank empties, its pressure drops, and the exit port for the stove must gradually be opened more and more to keep the gas flow at the desired level. Once the opening is at the maximum, the gas flow continues to weaken.

Cartridges also should be allowed to rest a few minutes before lighting them. If the butane has been "sloshing" around, it increases the pressure, and there is more likelihood of a flare-up when the stove is lit.

WHITE-GASOLINE STOVES

White-gasoline stoves use either white gasoline or the refined version of it called "stove and lantern fuel." These stoves come in two basic types, those without a pressure pump (self-generating units) and those with a pump.

With self-generating units, the heat of the burner transfers to the burner stem and keeps the fuel vaporized. A unit with a built-in pump relies on the pump to pressurize the fuel.

With most of the white gasoline stoves, the tank gets hot from reflected heat from the bottom of the pot and from the heat conducted down the burner stem. The tanks have a safety-release valve that's located in the filler cap. This safety-release valve is designed to blow before the tank gets hot enough to explode. If the valve blows, there is a burst of flame. So the safety valve should always be pointed in a safe direction.

The tank can dangerously overheat for a number of reasons: (1) using too large a pot, (2) running the unit dry, (3) including the fuel tank in a shroud or banking earth around it, or (4) running the stove too long. Aluminum foil can be used to reflect heat away from the fuel tank, but it's better to avoid overworking the stove.

PRIMING (PREHEATING)

With one exception (the Coleman 576), white gasoline stoves have to be preheated or primed in order to gain sufficient pressure. For this, there is a small cup or indentation around the base of the burner stem. Gasoline, alcohol, priming paste, or sterno can be placed in this cup and lit.

As the priming fuel begins to burn out, open the valve. Vaporized fuel should emerge, hit the dying flames of the priming fuel, and ignite around the burner plate. However, even with luck, you can succeed in lighting the stove from the dying flames of the primer only half of the time. Otherwise you'll need another match. If the fuel comes out in an unvaporized (liquid) stream, shut the unit off and prime it again.

There are many ways to prime a unit. Burning matches or paper can be held under the burner. Or the stove can be warmed in a hot sun for a few minutes. The idea is to pressurize the fuel, causing some vaporation. Though this requires heat, bear in mind that too much heat is a potential danger.

FUEL BOTTLES

White gasoline stoves have built-in fuel tanks ranging in size from 2 to 24 ounces. If you are going to need more fuel than the tank holds, you'll have to carry a reserve fuel bottle.

Fuel bottles and the stove's tank should be filled only 3-quarters full. Fuels expand with increases in altitude or surrounding temperature. The liquid fuel can exert great pressure and rupture a too-full bottle or tank. Pressure can also cause the fuel to spray from the bottle or tank as it is opened.

White gasoline, stove and lantern fuel, kerosene and alcohol weigh less than water. Backpackers calculating weights should figure that ¾ quart of white gas or stove and lantern fuel weighs about 24 ounces. The same volume of kerosene or alcohol weighs 27 ounces.

FIELD TESTS OF MAJOR STOVES

For a detailed report, refer to my comments in the appendix at the end of this book.

SELECTING A LIGHT-PACK STOVE

No one can really tell you what to buy or carry. This is a personal thing, but here are some basics that may prevent disappointments.

Before buying any stove based on recommendations of experienced backpackers or based on the results of the tests shown in the appendix, examine it. Is everything there? Are the instructions adequate? If not, get satisfaction. Look over the joints. Is everything "square"? Are the drill holes, especially the valve stem hole, centered? An off-center valve stem hole can mean a leaky valve. Does the key turn properly and easily? Does the unit disassemble as it should?

If a pot or pots are part of the package, are they of usable size to you? If not, they are extra weight and cost.

Butane units are very popular and useful. They can be used quite effectively in cool to hot temperatures. Disadvantages: (1) you should pack empty cartridges back to civilization with you; (2) cartridges are bulky; (3) costs of operating butane are high when compared to costs for white gasoline or kerosene.

The white gasoline or kerosene units with built-in pressure pumps are good at any altitude and in any weather. They can be heavy or extremely light (the M.S.R. 9A and M.S.R. MF stoves, for instance). But upon getting a new gasoline or kerosene stove home, you should flush the tank out with fuel—primarily to rid the unit of bits of welding.

Practice using the unit at home—*outdoors for safety*. "Burn it in" by boiling ½-dozen quarts of water, one at a time, allowing the stove to cool between boils. Get the feel of the unit.

With a white gasoline or kerosene unit, check to see if the flame centers on the burner plate. If not, wait until the unit is cool and make the adjustment.

A yellow, smoky flame means that any of the fuel types is burning improperly. Usually the stove needs more time to heat or it may need repriming. Any fuel that burns yellow leaves carbon (soot) on the burner. A clean burner burns better.

If there is something wrong with the unit, return it to the dealer. I've yet to meet a dealer, manufacturer, or distributor who wouldn't either correct the malfunction or exchange the unit.

WEIGHT

Be sure to consider the weight of the fuel you'll have to carry as well as the weight of the stove itself. Fuel requirements may make some stoves heavier, overall, than others of greater basic stove weight. Weights of fuel consumed are given in the Appendix "Test Report on Light-Pack Stoves."

POTS AND UTENSILS

Once you've become familiar with your stove, it's time to consider the pots. For maximum efficiency, the pots should: (1) be 7 inches in diameter, (2) have close fitting lids, (3) hold at least a quart (preferably two or three), (4) be lightweight, and (5) have blackened bottoms (to absorb heat).

The diameter of each pot is important. In my tests, the 7-inch pot was more efficient than smaller ones. At 8 inches, the pot begins to reflect heat back to the stove at a rate higher than considered acceptable from a safety standpoint.

The lid is important and should be used whenever possible. If you can't obtain a decent lid, you can substitute aluminum foil. Bore a hole of about ½ inch in the center of the foil to keep the water from bubbling over the sides. A lid keeps the air or cooling breezes from the surface of the water, and holds the heat in the pot.

If the pot holds less than a quart when full, it's going to be too small for much cooking. Some of the stoves tested came with pots as part of the package. These pots were quite small and seem to me of doubtful value.

The lighter the pot(s), the less weight you carry.

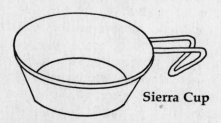

Sierra Cup

Blackened pot bottoms can speed the cooking by as much as 14 to 18 percent—with a fuel savings. Bottoms of pots can be blackened with stove polish, available at most hardware stores. Paint the stove polish onto the bottom of the pot, let it dry, and then sandpaper it lightly, making it as thin as possible without exposing metal, which would reflect heat. You want the pots to help absorb heat without being thick enough to act as insulation.

A Sierra cup can act as a very small pan. It will hold a bit more than one measuring cup of water.

A good plastic measuring cup is useful, and weighs less than a metal cup. Be certain that it's made of heat-durable plastic that won't melt when holding hot water or grease.

A wide-mouth, watertight, food-grade plastic container is useful for carrying leftovers from meals or prepared meals. It's also useful for rehydrating salads or soaking other dried foods before cooking.

Plastic squeeze tubes are about the easiest means for carrying butters, grease, jams, etc. They are available in most sporting goods and all backpacking stores.

A 4- or 8-ounce plastic baby bottle is good for carrying liquids and syrups. Reverse the nipple and screw the cap down for a watertight container.

Only a large spoon may be necessary, but a fork is better for blending dried foods with water. If you are using Teflon-lined pots, plastic forks and spoons may be worth considering. Metal may scratch the Teflon.

If you carry metal forks and spoons, you can eliminate some weight by shortening the handles. But this makes them more difficult to use.

A serrated plastic knife works well with food and is very light. But many people put their regular knife to use instead.

If you are going to fry foods, or make bannock, you may want to carry a small spatula. However, most fried foods can be turned with a fork or spoon.

Plastic Squeeze
Tube (p. 9)

There is much more equipment available, some of it suitable and some not. Avoid buying cheap equipment, however pretty it looks. And before taking something on the trail, try it at home. Maybe the pot's handle or bail is off balance, in which case you may lose an entire dinner.

You can, if necessary, get along with a lightweight lidded, aluminum pot from your kitchen. The handle can be cut off, or the rivets punched out and new rivets installed to fill the holes.

I find that one 2-quart lidded pot, a Sierra cup, a fork, and a spoon are often enough.

COOKING TECHNIQUES

OMB (ONE MINUTE BOIL)

What I call the OMB, One Minute Boil, is a variation on the frontier "hot box" or "fireless cooker." This method can save well over half the fuel many backpackers use.

When doing the OMB in a kitchen, you need a pot with a lid and an insulated box slightly larger than the pot. The food is brought to a boil, and boiled gently for from 1 to 10 minutes. Then the pot, still covered, is placed in the insulated box where it continues to cook for hours without the further application of heat.

Here's how to adapt this method to light-pack or survival cooking: (1) mix the dried foods with the required amount of water; (2) bring them to a boil, stirring as necessary, but leaving the lid on the pot as much as possible; (3) let the food boil gently for one minute, then remove from the heat and let it sit, still covered, until done. Normally with the foods described in this book, it takes 15 to 20 minutes.

If there is a wind, if the air is cold, or if you are above 5,000 feet, the heating process will likely have to be repeated once during the sit-time. If you are below 5,000 feet and it's a reasonably warm day, you may not have to reheat.

This method can be improved on with a homemade, insulated pot bag. Make it double the thickness and fill the space between with fiberglass insulation, available at hardware stores. It's easiest to slip this insulated pot bag *over* the pot rather than try and lower the pot *into* the bag. Naturally, the pot should sit on some sort of insulation.

With an insulated pot bag, a second application of heat should be unnecessary. And the bag can double in service by carrying your utensils on the trail.

That's all there is to it. Keep the lid on the pot, bring the food to a boil, let it boil gently for one minute, remove it from the heat, and let it sit until done.

MIXING DRIED AND GROUND INGREDIENTS WITH WATER

To keep lumps from forming and to speed the cooking, mix the ingredients properly. First put a little cold water into the pot. Add the ground food mixture and blend it with the water, adding water a bit at a time as needed. Do this slowly and well. When the food mix is creamy in texture, slowly add the balance of the water, stirring as you do.

STIRRING

When using a small stove, it's necessary to stir the dried mix from time to time, or it may stick to the bottom of the pot and burn.

GREASE

When frying with grease, don't let the grease become so hot that it smokes. Smoke means that the grease is burning. Burning grease gives an unpleasant taste to the food.

REHYDRATING DRIED FOODS

If the dried foods are going to be used later, they can be rehydrated by adding enough water to cover. When the foods are rehydrated, any excess water can be used or poured off. For some foods, such as beans, more water may be necessary.

With prepackaged trail foods, the amount of water needed for rehydration is noted on the package. But after some experimenting, you may wish to use more or less water than recommended.

With foods dried and packaged at home, it's generally best to add 4½ or more parts water to each part of dried mix for soups, and 3½ parts water for stews. Or the food can be weighed before drying and again after drying. The water that was removed by dehydration makes the difference. Add this weight of water, less 10 percent. (Very few foods rehydrate fully.)

It's not necessary to soak dried foods before cooking. However, if soaked, they take slightly less cooking time and have greater bulk (but no greater food value) when done.

RECIPES IN THIS BOOK

The recipes are intended to be packaged at home, labeled with type or content, and simply cooked until done, in most cases. They are designed to give from 18 to 20 ounces of cooked food, and serve as the main, perhaps only, dish eaten at a meal.

They can be increased or reduced as you please. They may be cooked using the OMB (One Minute Boil) I described earlier or simply cooked until done.

BOILING

One more word on cooking techniques. Once the boiling point is reached, the water temperature never gets any hotter, regardless of increased application of heat. So there is no reason to keep the flame any higher than necessary to barely keep the water boiling. Lowering the flame to the minimum necessary helps you economize on fuel.

PART
II

HOME PREPARATION

DRYING FOODS

Many foods can be purchased dried. Some are normal grocery or delicatessen items, and others are specially prepared trail foods. There are four drying processes usually used. They are air drying, heat or sun drying, vacuum drying, and freeze drying.

Air drying is done by simply exposing the food to dry air and letting it leech the moisture out of the food.

Heat or sun drying can be done in a dehydrator or in the sun. Most dried fruits purchased at a grocery are sun dried.

Vacuum drying exposes the food to a vacuum and lets the vacuum leech the moisture out.

Freeze drying is a process called "vacuum sublimation." The fresh or freshly cooked foods are flash frozen, put into a large vacuum chamber, and the air is removed. They are then subjected to radiant heat. The extreme temperature difference causes the water to turn, almost instantly, to steam which is sucked out by the vacuum pumps, leaving the dried food.

HEAT DRYING AND DEHYDRATORS

The foods you dry yourself are the least expensive and often the best tasting. Here, savings over buying foods ready-dried can run from 70 to 100 percent. Leftovers, that might otherwise be thrown away, can be dried and carried on the trail. Dried meats (not just jerky, but most types of meats) cost about 20 percent of the price of commercially dried meats. Similar percentages of savings hold true for almost all foods.

Fully cooked, dried foods are excellent fare. They can be prepared as part of normal dinner preparations and dried later. These can be rehydrated without heat and eaten cold, if necessary. They are very useful at higher altitudes, where the water boils at too low a temperature to permit adequate heating and, thus, cooking.

To begin, you don't have to buy a special dehydrator, for you can use your oven. Even though a kitchen oven is a very small dehydrator compared to commercial models, it is an excellent one.

Set the temperature between 120 and 140°F. If possible, check it with a thermometer. All properly prepared foods will dry between these two temperatures, and usually dry overnight, leaving the oven free for normal use. At lower temperatures, some foods will sour, and at higher temperatures, some will burn rather quickly.

The humidity in the air will affect the drying rate. On very humid days, the drying takes longer than on dry days. Cracking open the oven door helps allow some of the moist air in the oven to escape.

The oven racks can be used to support food mats. Good mat materials include: (1) fiberglass screen, available at hardware stores; (2) nylon netting, available in groceries and yard goods stores; (3) cheesecloth, available at groceries; or (4) baking trays. The first three types of mats are easily attached to the racks with clothespins.

Put the prepared foods on the covered racks or trays. Spread them one layer deep and set the oven to 130°F (120 to 140°F). Close door and let the food dry.

Foods with heavy odors should be dried separately as the odor will transfer to the other foods that are drying. An extreme example of this would be drying strawberries and chopped onions at the same time. The air flow would contaminate the strawberries with the onion taste.

Food is drying properly when it feels slightly cooler than the air around it. Temperature can be turned down if the food feels slightly warm. The food is "dry" when it is hard or brittle, or in some cases, leathery. This and the proper preparation of food are discussed later in this book in greater detail.

While the kitchen oven is an excellent dehydrator, you can make a special dehydrator or purchase one.

The simplest dehydrator is made with a 60-watt light bulb, a couple of bricks, an oven tray or shelf, and a corrugated cardboard box. Position the light bulb off the surface of

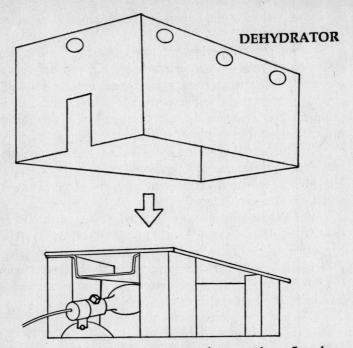

a table. Arrange the bricks to support the tray about 5 inches above the bulb, and put some sort of shield between the bulb and the tray: a piece of cardboard that doesn't touch either is good. This shield should be about four times the size of the bulb. It serves two purposes: (1) it keeps water from falling onto the bulb; and (2) it helps distribute the heat from the bulb.

Then put the food on the rack. Punch some ½-inch holes around the bottom of the box. Put the box over the whole affair, bottom up, and switch on the bulb. The dehydrator is working.

Small commercially made dehydrators are available in many stores and by mail order from a number of sources (see page 185).

Two that have served me well—and which I highly recommend—are the Dri-Mor Dehydrator and the Zephyr.

The Dri-Mor Dehydrator will hold up to about 20 pounds of food. It has a fan and a thermostat. It is well made of aluminum and very efficient.

The Zephyr is larger, holding up to about 45 pounds of food. It has a fan, a thermostat, and a temperature control. The Zephyr is made of wood and from the outside appears to be a fine piece of furniture. Because the Zephyr is compartmentalized, you can dry six drastically different foods at one time.

GRINDING

There are many reasons for grinding food. Some packaged foods are far bulkier than necessary. Some foods need grinding to speed their cooking, and some foods need grinding to mix them with other foods or to hasten the drying process.

A food grinder does the best job. If you don't have one, a kitchen blender is a reasonably satisfactory substitute.

CONCENTRATING LIQUIDS

This technique has been used for hundreds, perhaps thousands, of years to reduce the bulk of some "traveler's foods."

Put the liquid in a pan and reduce it by simmering over heat. Reduce it until it's fairly thick. In this manner, a pint (16 ounces) of most liquids can be reduced easily to an ounce or two.

Next pour the reduced liquid into a fairly thin china or plastic cup. (Metal or pottery gives an unpleasant taste.) Set the cup in a pan of water and bring the water to a light simmer. The liquid in the cup will slowly reduce to a thick, glue-like substance as the water simmers.

Further reduction or concentration can be done by letting this concentrate sit exposed to air, or by drying it in an oven or dehydrator. It's best, with the least chance of mold, to mix the concentrate with a little cornstarch and roll it into very small pellets. Dry these in the oven or dehydrator, or leave them in a warm, dry kitchen. These air-dry quickly. Once dried, they should be ground into a flour.

Normally, 8 ounces of water are added to ½ ounce of the concentrated powder. If less is added, the resulting liquid will be richer. If more is added, the results will be thinner. You'll also have to apply heat. Bring the water and concentrate to a boil, and let it sit 10 minutes, covered.

SATURATING DRIED FOODS

This is a technique that I came up with some years ago. It gives an excellent and very rich gravy that's built right into the food. It can also be used to make foods, such as beans or potatoes, taste like beefsteak, or it can be used to make apples or rice taste like oranges, and so forth.

There are two slightly different methods of saturating foods. Which to use depends on the type of food to be saturated.

For uncooked dried foods, such as beans, lentils, millet, and barley, foods that are normally presoaked before cooking, presoak them in the saturating liquid. Then fully cook them, using the same liquid instead of water. When they are fully cooked, they will be saturated with the liquid. Then simply dry them.

For instance, 1 pound of beans will absorb four cans of concentrated beef bouillon. When dried, this blend will weigh a couple of ounces more than it did before cooking (the weight of the dried beef bouillon). When they are rehydrated, the four cans of beef bouillon are also rehydrated.

Another instance, rice can be cooked in concentrated beef or chicken bouillon and then dried.

Often these saturated dried foods are so well saturated that you may want to mix 1 part saturated and 1 part unsaturated to soften the intense taste.

To saturate foods prepared from fresh foods, dry the food properly and then rehydrate it in the liquid you want to saturate it with. Once rehydrated, it is saturated and is dried again.

This is a simple and effective technique that results in an easy-to-prepare, rich dish.

MAKING LEATHERS

"Leather" is a term often used to describe dried fruit purees that feel like sheets of leather and taste like ambrosia.

I first made leathers by drying gravies before grinding them and by making strips of meat ground together with a moist filler that, when cooked, increased significantly in bulk.

The method has two uses, one to produce a finished product and the other as one stage of a drying process for purees.

To make a leather, simply puree the ingredients. Run them through a blender until they are the consistency of tomato sauce (sauce, not paste) and pour them on a plastic film (wrap) covered tray. Tilt the puree and tray a bit to spread the puree evenly over the tray, about ⅛-inch thick.

Put the tray into an oven or dehydrator and dry it. Fruit purees can be dried in the sun; others should not. If you are sun drying fruit puree, use a cheesecloth cover to keep flies away.

If you use an oven or dehydrator, wait until the puree is dry enough to lift from the tray, remove the plastic film, and complete the drying on the racks. Some types of puree, such as gravies, will crack and break up when removed.

To fully dry a gravy, it's usually necessary to take it up when it feels dry, cut it into small pieces, and grind the pieces. Put the grounds back on the tray and finish the drying. Grind again when they are fully dry.

Leathers are easily dried at 130°F.

DRYING COMMERCIALLY CANNED FOODS

Some canned foods can be dried. The main problem (storage after drying) is the fat used in canning. For instance, to dry a can of chili con carne and beans, heat the contents well and let this sit in the refrigerator until cool. After the fat has risen to the surface, remove it.

This heating and chilling process should be repeated. Once most, or all, of the fat is removed, spread the contents on a tray and commence drying. Be sure to spread the ingredients thinly and evenly first. Several times during the drying process, check and respread the food again to ensure that the heat has hit each particle of food.

If there is a great deal of fat, such as in canned corn beef hash, drying is inadvisable because the dried food becomes rancid too quickly.

It is best to weigh the food before drying and again afterward. The weight lost—less 10 percent—is the weight of water to be added to rehydrate.

The thickeners used in canning usually do not stay effective after the drying, so you should add a thickener to the dried food.

THICKENERS

You will often want to thicken a dish. Stews and some other dishes are not quite right without a thickener. There are five or six commonly used thickeners for home cooking. They are flour, cornstarch (and other starches), various types of vegetables and grains (such as potatoes, cornmeal, masa harina), egg yolks, and tapioca.

With light-pack foods, cornstarch is the easiest thickener to use. It thickens quickly, without a long application of heat. A tablespoonful thickens 1½ to 2 cups of liquid.

You can mix the cornstarch right in with the other ingredients of your dried mix. Caution: Avoid adding too much thickener. You can always add more on the trail. But it's impossible to remove. Excess thickener requires thinning the dish with water.

If you are going to add more cornstarch to a dish that's heated, blend the cornstarch with cold water before adding it.

If you blend it right into the hot dish or with hot water, it lumps badly.

Instant mashed potatoes can be used to thicken a dish, but they produce more of a potato mush than a sauce.

So far I've talked about thickeners that require cooking. There are several that do not need cooking, and they will thicken a dish that is cold, for instance, a dessert or milkshake.

The two that are most easily available are *Gum Tragacanth* and *Sodium Alginate*. Sodium Alginate is easily available at a health food store. Gum Tragacanth can be obtained from a druggist.

Sodium Alginate is a derivative from Kelp. It's also used in many instant puddings on the grocery shelf.

One teaspoon will thicken 8 ounces of liquid. Stir in a little liquid and mix well, then add the balance of the liquid, stirring as you do. Let it sit for a few minutes.

SIZING FOOD TO BE DRIED

This is covered in individual sections of this book, but a good rule of thumb is to make small pieces of uniform size. If you try to dry different sizes at the same time, the smaller will dry before the larger. Most pieces should be from ¼- to ½-inch thick, whether sliced or diced. Rice is about the smallest particle food used for cooked-and-dried foods. It requires no sizing, and it's about the fastest drying. It also rehydrates fast (see rice listings in the index).

PACKAGING

Properly packaged dried foods can cut backpack bulk considerably. Commercially prepared dried foods are usually packed for a shelf life of 5 years or more. This requires airtight and lightproof packaging that is heavier and bulkier than practical for the pack.

For example, 15 or more 1-pint freezer bags and sealers

weigh less than the packaging around a one 4-ounce package of freeze-dried food.

It's usually best to package by the dish and by the meal, then label the contents, note the amounts of water to be added, note other cooking information, and identify what is in the package.

Freezer bags are easy to obtain and use. They are dependable and are made of a good-grade plastic. Plastic sandwich bags often give way at the seams. Freezer bags come in pint, quart, and larger sizes. Use a size somewhat larger than the food load, smooth it out after the food is in, and seal tightly with rubber bands or the sealers that come with the bags. Cut excess bag off.

It's best if the package is flexible and not stuffed, but in either case, exhaust as much air as possible.

Plastic medicine containers make good vials for items such as spices.

Plastic "squeeze tubes" are excellent containers for butters and grease. They look like toothpaste tubes with the bottom open. To fill them you spoon the food in through the open bottom. Then you seal the bottom with a slotted plastic tube.

Liquids are easily carried in 4- or 8-ounce plastic baby bottles. By reversing the nipple and screwing the lid and cap down, you make a watertight container.

Foods from the grocery or delicatessen usually should be repackaged.

Another method of reducing bulk is to add ground foods to a package. For instance, you can fill the spaces between packaged beans with dried and ground refried beans, or you can fill the spaces between dried corn with cornmeal. Other possibilities depend on what foods you decide to carry.

When cooking, you can either separate the filler and use it some other time, or you can add enough water and use it in the dish. If you use it in the dish, you are "extending" the food, as home economists term it.

Freeze-dried foods can be extended to cut their average cost. As an example, a package of freeze-dried beef stew can be extended by adding more dried potatoes or vegetables.

The most compact freeze-dried foods are the compressed discs. While fairly expensive, they save from 26 to 37 percent of the space used by regular packaged freeze-dried foods. Before being carried, they should be repackaged. The commercial package takes up a great deal of pack space.

Despite some instructions to the contrary, it's not a good idea to burn any plastic. Some plastic and some plastic containers give off very unpleasant, even deadly, fumes when burned. If you feel that you must burn plastic, stay well upwind. The best policy is to pack home such items.

STORING DRIED FOODS

Dried foods should be packaged as soon as possible after drying. Otherwise they will leech moisture out of the air. Once packaged, they should be kept cool, dark, and dry. Keep them in the coolest area you can. As a minimum, keep them out of sunlight as much as possible, and keep them dry. Heat, sunlight, and moisture can ruin even canned foods.

SHELF LIFE (LENGTH OF STORAGE)

Foods dried at the temperatures recommended in this book, 130°F (120 to 140°F), will keep from 8 to 24 months, depending on ingredients and storage. Exactly how long any one food (fresh, canned, frozen, or dried) will keep depends on the storage conditions.

Later in the book, I note the "shelf life" of various foods. These rough estimates are based on constant, very warm or hot weather, with proper packaging and storage. And the figures are conservative. Foods will normally last longer.

To repeat, for the longest shelf life, food should be kept as dry and as cool as possible, and out of sunlight.

READING THE LABELS

When you buy commercially packaged foods, what actually is in them? What is their actual food value? Usually the answer to this is on the labels.

INGREDIENTS

There is usually a section on the label listing the ingredients. The rule is that the ingredients are listed in order of weight. This is true of foods prepared in the United States. Food from other countries may not have useful labels.

If the first item on the label is beef, then the package contains more beef, by weight, than any other one ingredient. If the first item on the label is cornstarch, then the package contains more cornstarch, by weight, than any other ingredient.

Here are the lists of ingredients (other than water) from two brands of "beef stock."

1. "Hydrolyzed Plant Protein, Autolysed Yeast Extract, Salt, Beef Extract, Flavoring, Sugar, Vegetable Gum and Caramel Coloring." (This costs 23 cents an ounce.)
2. "Beef Stock, Hydrolyzed Beef Protein, Hydrolyzed Vegetable Protein, Extract of Beef, Yeast Extract, Salt, Sugar, Caramel Coloring, Corn Starch and Spices." (This costs 28 cents an ounce.)

Item 1 comes in a very fancy bottle, but it tastes like a weak oatmeal. Item 2 comes in a plain bottle, but tastes like real beef.

FOOD-VALUE ANALYSIS

On food labels, the value and analyses are often printed in very small type. But if you can read them, they are fairly easy to understand. They are usually given in percentages of dry weight, and variations are usually explained.

Sometimes you will need to convert grams to ounces, since both may be used on one label. This practice seems to be purposefully confusing. Just remember that 1 ounce equals 28 grams (actually 28.35 grams). This way, if a label says "25% protein," you are getting 7 grams of protein per ounce.

Sometimes a breakfast food label will have the above information. But on looking closer, you may find that it says "with one-half cup of milk." In this case, you have to deduct the food value of ½ cup of milk. This varies slightly from area to area, but is generally around 18 calories and 1 gram of protein per ounce, or 72 calories and 4 grams of protein per ½ cup (4 ounces).

It's worth noting that what is in the package may differ from what is on the label. Production changes, altered recipes, or imprecise measurement can affect nutritional values. In fact, due to natural variables, ingredients of equal weight may vary in food value: Two grains of corn may offer slightly different actual food values.

MEATS, FISH AND MEAT SUBSTITUTES

HEAT-DRIED MEATS

"To dry meat take lean meat and slice it in thin strips, then dip it in hot brine and hang it in the kitchen to dry."

from recipe book handwritten about 1830

You can heat dry the following: (1) raw meat with blood, (2) raw meat with the blood removed (deblooded), (3) corned meats, and (4) fully cooked meats.

If you heat dry raw meat with blood, it will not rehydrate. This is the jerky that is usually sold commercially. The more blood that is drawn from the meat before drying, the faster and more complete the rehydration. Uncooked corned or pickled meats will rehydrate, somewhat, after drying because the pickling process reduces the blood in the meat.

Fully cooked meats almost fully rehydrate after being heat dried.

Stone age people removed the blood from their meats by pounding the meat with a rock under water. They also dried their meat in or near a fire, or by a combination of sun and wind.

It is easy to remove the blood from fresh meat. Slice the meat for drying and put it in a bowl of water. Then squeeze the blood from it. This requires several changes of water. When the meat is fully deblooded, it is white in color.

Blood has food value, but also weight. Deblooded meats are lighter, and though they have less food value per ounce, there is still significant food value in them.

HEAT DRYING RAW MEAT

1. Types of meat: You can use beef, lamb, horse, buffalo, game, snake, goat, fish, fowl, pork. (Caution: If using pork, let the pork sit in a freezer for at least twenty days, at zero degrees or less, before drying. This eliminates the danger of Trichinosis, or tapeworm.) If you butcher your own meat, be certain it is from a healthy animal.

2. Use the leanest meat that you can find and then trim all visible fat from it. Don't use well marbled meat for drying. Fats add an unpleasant taste and turn rancid fairly quickly.

3. Cut the meat into thin strips, with or against the grain, or on a bias. If cut with the grain, the jerky will be slightly tougher than if cut against the grain. The meat should be sliced in uniform strips from ⅛- to ¼-inch thick. The thinner the slices, the quicker the drying. (If you are going to dip the meat in hot brine, it should be somewhat thicker— about ½ inch.)

4. Dip the sliced meat into a brine or work a dry brine into it. This adds shelf life and flavor to the jerky. Salt inhibits bacterial growth and helps preserve the meat. If the

meat is not brined it's still good, but the shelf life is considerably shorter, sometimes as short as a month or two.

PLAIN BRINE

One-half cup of salt to 1 quart of water will produce a brine that will "float an egg." This is an old recipe for brine. And it's excellent. If you dip the meat into this brine when the brine is hot (slightly smoking), the meat will turn grey as it partially cooks. The dipping time should be about 1 minute. This brined meat can be hung to dry in a warm, dry place in the kitchen. If there are flies around, sprinkle the meat with pepper to keep them off. The meat should dry in a day or so in the kitchen and become excellent jerky. Brined meat, as above, can be dried in an oven or dehydrator at 130°F. Here it will normally dry in 3 to 5 hours.

SEASONED BRINE

Seasoning can be added to jerky brines. Some favorites are garlic, lemon, powdered sage (which may make the meat taste like sausage), liquid smoke, onion, chili, a spoonful or two of hickory smoked salt.

Soy sauce can also be substituted for the salt. Add 1 cup of soy sauce to a quart of water. The soy sauce contains salt and sugar. The sweetness of the sugar is almost irresistible to flies, and if you use soy sauce instead of salt, it's best to dry the meat in the oven or dehydrator, not hung up in the kitchen.

DRY BRINE

Dry brine can be simply a layer of salt rubbed into the meat.

The meat may also be buried in salt, each piece covered with salt and separated from other pieces by more salt. Let this sit for a day or two and then dry it. This method results in a very salty, sometimes too salty, meat.

You can air-dry dry-brined meat, or you can use an oven or dehydrator. If dried at 120 to 140°F, it takes from 5 to 10 hours to dry, depending on the thickness of the meat, the amount of blood, and humidity. The jerky is adequately dry when it bends slightly before cracking.

Corned beef jerky is made by using regular uncooked corned (pickled) beef, trimming all visible fat, slicing the beef, and drying it. It's not necessary to give it a brine treatment for a long shelf life. After being dried, this can be eaten as a snack (it's very salty) or ground and used in corned beef hash and other cooked dishes. Since it has been pickled, it will rehydrate fairly well.

You can get meat pellets by asking the butcher to run lean meat through a chili grinder once. This results in ¼-inch strings of meat. Deblood, brine, and dry. Break into small pieces for use in cooking.

Powdered jerky is simply dried meat run through a grinder or blender until it is a powder. This makes excellent broth when added to boiling water. A good mix is 1 cup (8 ounces) of water to each ounce of dried and ground jerky.

RAW-MEAT LEATHERS

Making leather is an interesting method of preparing raw-meat jerky for cooking.

Have lean meat ground twice and remove the blood. The ground meat will crumble under water as you do this. Soak it briefly, no more than a minute in cool brine. Spread the meat thinly on a tray covered with plastic film (wrap) and dry it at 130°F. When finished, it will come off the plastic film mainly in small pieces, but a few will be as large as a hand. Cut the large pieces into smaller ones and use them in cooking.

Oatmeal or a Textured Vegetable Protein (TVP) can be added to the meat. Add the oatmeal or TVP and some water to the meat. Run the mixture through a blender until it is a thick puree. Pour the puree on the plastic film and dry it.

Adding oatmeal or TVP to the meat adds bulk when the dried meat is rehydrated in cooking.

HEAT DRYING FULLY COOKED MEATS

This is probably the most practical part of this meat section because it provides an alternative for leftovers—which can become excellent foods. Cooked meats rehydrate well after being dried. And fully cooked meats need not undergo a brine treatment.

If possible, let the cooked meat sit overnight in the refrigerator. This makes it easier to remove the visible fat. Raw (unrefined) meat fats turn rancid quickly.

Remove the fat, cut the meat into small pieces—½-inch squares or ¼-inch strips. With most roasts, including chicken and turkey, fairly long, thin strips of meat can be pulled from them when they are cool. Roasts make excellent dried meats, and offer an interesting menu change.

If the meat has been basted in fat or is fatty, as chicken and turkey often are, it should be dipped in boiling water for a minute or two to rid it of the fat before drying.

Roasts can be planned that have little fat. They can be partially eaten at dinner and then cut up for drying. They can be cooked without fat. Here you can remove a piece for drying and then pour fatty gravy over the dinner portion.

Put the cut or sliced meat on a tray or netting and dry it at 130°F. It will dry fairly fast. When cooked meat is dry, it is very light and feels like a bundle of dried fibers.

GROUND MEAT FOR DRYING

Ground meats and meatballs should be specially prepared for drying because almost all "store" ground meat has fat. If you cannot obtain lean ground meat, use the best you can find. After drying it, package it in an airtight container and store in the freezer until you are ready to take it with you. It will usually keep for several weeks or more after removal from the freezer. Here's a recipe for drying meat or meatballs:

31

1   pound completely lean meat ground twice
½   c of oatmeal
1   medium sized onion chopped very fine
        (or 2 T minced dried onions)
¼   t pepper
1   t salt
1   large egg
¾   c of water

Sprinkle the oatmeal over the meat and then mix all the ingredients together completely. (You can use bread-crumbs or TVP, but oatmeal works and seems to taste best.) Let this sit ½ hour or so and then roll into ½-inch meatballs and boil them in water until done. Pressure cooking is fast and convenient. Use 15 pounds pressure for 4 to 5 minutes and then cool immediately. Run cold water over the pressure cooker. Caution: *Do not* open the cooker until it has cooled.

After draining the meatballs, spread them on a tray or netting, and then dry them. These can be used as meatballs, but they work better if crushed by hand and used as hamburger. For meatballs, allow at least 10 minutes of soaking after heat's applied. Adding oatmeal results in greater bulk in rehydration.

This type of dried hamburger is excellent when used with the various grocery packages of dried ingredients that call for hamburger. Add 5 or 6 ounces of this dried meat to a pint or so of water and let it rehydrate. Or bring the water to a boil and put the dried meat into it. This should be allowed to sit off the heat for 15 minutes. Then add enough water to make up the amount appropriate for the dried food mix. Give this a One Minute Boil (OMB) plus a sit-time of 15 to 20 minutes, or simply cook until done.

PEMMICAN

Pemmican is an American Indian word (Cree) meaning "fat meat." Today, pemmican is generally thought of as a fruit, nut, and meat bar. The term is also misused occasionally to describe a bar similar to a fruit cake.

Pemmican—fat meat—is very useful, easy to make, and high in calories and protein. The staple ingredients are ground jerky and fat. The easiest fats to use are lard or vegetable shortening. The lard results in better tasting pemmican because lard accents the taste of the food. Vegetable shortening makes a slightly harder pemmican. Pemmican can be flavored to taste.

Good results are obtained using well ground cooked and dried meat. This is because the meat will rehydrate when cooked, giving a little more bulk and making it easier to chew.

Ounce for ounce commercial meat bars (pemmican) sell for five times what homemade pemmican costs. To shape the pemmican into bars, pack it into a large match box lined with plastic film (wrap), then remove.

BASIC PEMMICAN

2 oz cooked, ground, and dried beef
2½ oz lard or vegetable fat (shortening)

Put the meat in the container, lined with plastic film. Melt the fat and let it cool slightly to a gluey consistency. Pour the fat over the meat and let it harden. Wrap airtight and store, preferably in a freezer if you won't need the pemmican for many weeks.

PEMMICAN NO. 2

2 oz cooked, ground, and dried beef
2½ oz lard or vegetable fat
1 T minced dried onions
Prepare as above.

PEMMICAN NO. 3

2 oz cooked, ground, and dried beef
3 oz lard or vegetable fat
½ oz dried (heat-dried) ground berries
Prepare as above.

If pemmican is the basis of your foods, or if it's all that's being carried, then the ingredients added have a reason for being there. If the pemmican is just one item carried, as it usually is today, then berries and other additives are probably best carried separately.

The pemmican can be lightly salted. This should be done by gently sprinkling over the pemmican bar after it cools. Pepper can also be used.

Pemmican has a high food value. Made as the basic pemmican, above, it has 185 calories, 10 grams of protein, and 15 grams of fat *per ounce*.

Pemmican, like all dried foods, should be wrapped airtight and protected from light and heat. The shelf life is rather long, depending on ingredients, preparation, and storage conditions. Lard or vegetable shortening will last for a year or longer under normal conditions. Cooked and dried meat should last 8 months or more, properly prepared and stored. Cooked and dried meat covered with longlasting, clarified fat acquires added shelf life.

BACON

Bacon slabs can be carried. They should be used fairly soon, in a week if the weather is warm. In very hot weather, bacon should be used within a few days. It should also be protected from heat as much as possible, and it should be kept dry and out of sunlight.

Rubbing vinegar on bacon slabs helps preserve them by inhibiting the growth of mold.

Bacon slabs purchased at a meat counter often have received only a mild cure and may have water added to it. You can further salt cure slab bacon. Simply work a good portion of salt into every nook and cranny. Let it sit a week or so in the refrigerator, adding salt as necessary. The bacon will "bleed," so it should be placed on paper in a plate before being placed in the refrigerator.

This curing bacon should not sit in its own liquids any longer than necessary. You will have to change the paper and add salt periodically. It takes about a week for the salt to penetrate 1 inch of bacon, so if the piece is 2 inches thick, it will take about 2 weeks.

Another way to cure the slab is to first cut it into small, one-use pieces. After rubbing salt into them, bury them in salt for a week. Remove and brush the salt off. Package tightly, still with a thin layer of salt, and store in a freezer until taking it on the trail.

Bacon treated like this will normally last many weeks. These bacon slabs are "dehydrated."

Uncooked bacon is available in cans, usually 1-pound cans. Once the can has been opened, this bacon should be treated like fresh bacon, and not kept in the can. Expect canned bacon to last only a day or two in very hot weather.

Cooked and crumbled bacon is available in small (2 to 3 ounce) cans. Cooked and crumbled bacon, often mixed with preservatives, is available in 3-ounce pemmican bars.

Bacon can be cooked at home for packing. To save bulk, cook it with a flat weight on it to keep it flat. Cook until good and crisp, then stack neatly and cover with lard or a good vegetable shortening. It should last many weeks.

Textured Vegetable Protein (TVP) bacon is sold under various names. While this is easy to carry, it tastes only a bit like bacon.

If nothing else is available, a bacon taste can be had by using a *little* hickory smoked salt.

SAUSAGE

Sausage is available in soft or hard varieties. The only ones normally carried are the hard sausages. They will keep without refrigeration.

There are many varieties of hard sausage, from pepperonis and landjaegers to salami. Each manufacturer has its own recipes. Often the sausage will vary slightly in taste from one maker to another. Hard sausages are sometimes made without garlic and without many spices. These are good for packing if and when you can find them.

Buy hard sausage in 1- to 4-ounce chubs (pieces), rather than in large sticks. Some very small and inexpensive sausages are made with open ends. These are not recommended for outdoor use in warm weather because they can spoil in a few days.

Hard sausages get harder with age. They will also "bleed" through their casings. This is natural oil being drawn out of them, and the phenomenon is perfectly normal. However, this oil should not be eaten; it can cause bowel problems.

Use a hard sausage as you would any meat. Cut it into thin slices and use it in such dishes as stews, chowders, pastas, beans, with potatoes and with rice. Or eat it as a snack.

In continuous, very hot weather, you should use hard sausage within ten days. In normal weather, it will last for many months. To avoid mold, it should be carried so that air can circulate around it on occasion.

FREEZE-DRIED MEATS

Freeze-dried meats are available in many types: steaks, chops, chunks of cooked meats, hamburger, meatballs, and fish. Freeze-dried meats do not shrink as much as heat-dried meats, so they actually rehydrate considerably faster than heat-dried meat.

When using freeze-dried meats, remember that the instructions on some packages are slightly inaccurate. Some packages of hamburger patties instruct you to soak them for 5 minutes before cooking. These actually need 10 or even 15 minutes of soaking. Chops and steaks should usually be soaked for 15 to 20 minutes. If you do not soak freeze-dried meats long enough, you will dine on a very tough piece of cooked meat.

Some freeze-dried meats should be soaked and then removed from the water and allowed to stand awhile. After soaking, while standing, the fibers of the meat absorb the water more completely. Then the cooked product looks and tastes more like fresh meat.

FISH FOR THE PACK

You have a choice of purchasing freeze-dried, air-dried, or heat-dried fish or of drying your own. Freeze-dried fish are excellent. If you can find them and afford them, it's the most tasty way to have dried fish in your pack.

Usually freeze-dried fish are packaged in complete freeze-dried dinners, so it is difficult to find just the freeze-dried fish. However, when you do, it's worth stockpiling for future use.

Groceries, including oriental markets, will usually have dried cod (Finan Haddie), dried shrimp, dried cuttlefish, and dried bonita flakes. These generally have a concentrated flavor and should be used somewhat sparingly. The bonita flakes are used for a fish broth, the others are eaten as snacks. They will usually rehydrate slightly when cooked if they are ground a bit, or are sliced thinly.

They need a couple of hours of soaking prior to cooking, but even if not soaked and only sliced thin, they add flavor to the dish.

DRYING YOUR OWN FISH

Drying fish is as simple as drying meat. The same rules apply. Clean the fish well, and cut it into usable sections after removing all visible fat and blood—then brine it well and dry it. The pieces should be from ¼- to ½-inch thick.

For the trail, avoid using fattier fish such as trout and herring. As a strictly arbitrary limit, I have set 1 percent fat content as the limit for suitable fish for drying and packaging. In order from the least fat to almost 1 percent, the fish are as follows: (1) haddock, (2) scallops, (3) cod, (4) abalone, (5) seabass, (6) tilefish, (7) flounder, (8) cuttlefish, (9) shrimp, (10) sole, (11) burlot, (12) hard-shelled clams—soft-shelled have 2½ percent fat, (13) pollock, and (14) red or grey snapper.

It's worth noting here that the U.S. Bureau of Commercial Fisheries, of the Interior Department's U.S. Fish and Wildlife Service, writes of drying (home drying) fish with up to 5 percent fat content in Fishery Leaflet No. 18. The same leaflet advises "Cured fish . . . should be held at temperatures below 70 degrees."

If you are 20 or 30 miles out and backpacking on a warm day, the reduced fat content reduces the chance of spoilage and is a good idea. If at any time you think that your fish (or any food) might be spoiled, don't taste it. Just get rid of it and wash your hands well—to be safe.

TEXTURED VEGETABLE PROTEIN (TVP) AND EXTENDERS

These are usually the vegetarian meats and extenders found in markets and health food stores. However, there are some that will have real meat flavorings. You will have to read the ingredients on the package to find out.

TVP is available in small pieces and chunks. The chunks range in size from ½ to 1 inch. TVP is normally available in ham, sausage, bacon, beef, and chicken flavors. In stews and other dishes, they are used as you would use any meat. You have to add water to the dish to compensate for the water they absorb. They are light to carry, give a good increase in cooked bulk and weight, and are inexpensive. Their tastes are somewhat like, but not really the same as, meat.

Health food stores and sometimes grocery stores have a number of premixed types, such as FRITINI. The premixes have flavorings added and usually need be mixed only with water; an occasional egg is used as a binder. They are then ready to fry or cook. If you are going to use premixes and wish to use egg as a binder—use rehydrated dried eggs.

There are some premixed TVPs that are specifically made as additions and extenders to restaurant meat loaves.

They are available at restaurant supply stores. They can also be used just as they are in stews and chili. Some extenders add enough taste to the dish so you don't need other flavorings. Just read the package directions.

Here's an excellent recipe for a TVP "hamburger"

1   c beef flavored TVP (small pieces)
1¼ c water
1   t dried minced onion
1   T flour or ground oatmeal
2   eggs (dried)
salt and pepper

Mix the eggs with the required amount of water and let them sit. Mix the other ingredients together, and let them sit until all the water is absorbed. Then mix the eggs into the other ingredients, mash all ingredients well, and form into patties. Allow to stand 15 minutes or so—then fry in grease or oil.

CANNED MEATS AND FISH

These are about 50 percent water. In cans, they don't qualify as light-pack foods. But for short trips, the small cans are convenient, inexpensive, and often carried.

Small cans of foods such as deviled ham, liver pate, and sardines are often packed in aluminum and weigh around 3 ounces each. There is usually oil in the cans, good for snacks and cooking. In hot weather, use the contents at one sitting; they can spoil in an hour or two.

TOFU (SOY BEAN CAKE/CHEESE)

This is an oriental food that will absorb the taste of almost anything it is cooked with. It is made of soy flour and water with occasional seasonings.

Tofu is available dried in oriental markets. There are two basic forms of the dried versions. One is freeze-dried and the other is heat-dried. The freeze-dried comes in small cakes about ½-inch thick and rehydrates with the texture of a sponge. Tofu that has been frozen has a sponge texture, and there is no way to change it.

The heat-dried Tofu comes in thin sheets. After being soaked in water, it can be used in cooking. If you soak one and gently fry it in bacon grease, it will taste like bacon.

These are relatively high in calories and protein (106 calories and 11.5 grams protein per dry ounce) and, though unusual, are an excellent and longlasting light-pack food.

MUSHROOM AND NUTS AS MEAT SUBSTITUTES

If you want mushrooms, dry your own—they will be less expensive and probably best tasting. To dry them, simply clean them, remove the stems, and dry them.

Old recipes often call for walnuts and cashews as meat substitutes. Any edible nut will taste reasonably good in place of meat in almost any dish. Salted and roasted peanuts are good in chili and beans, and a lot less expensive than meat.

OLIVES AS MEAT SUBSTITUTES

Any brined olive, black or green, if pitted, will dry easily. The inexpensive cans of sliced olives dry quickly. If you are drying whole pitted olives, it speeds the drying to slice them in half.

Substitute for meat using 2 ounces of dried olives for every ounce of dried meat.

VEGETABLES

There is a choice of purchasing freeze-dried or commercially heat-dried vegetables. Or you can dry your own. It's a matter of taste, convenience, and cost.

The freeze-dried are the most expensive. But they have the best texture and body if you are going to eat them without cooking, such as in a vegetable salad. If you are going to cook your vegetables, freeze-dried and heat-dried versions offer similar results. Normally, freeze-dried vegetables are about twice as bulky as heat-dried. The compressed freeze-dried are slightly less bulky than heat-dried, but when compressed they lose some of their texture.

Groceries often have small cans of heat-dried vegetable flakes. This is the most expensive and least satisfactory way of buying them. Most commercially heat-dried vegetables have a slight taste of preservative. Freeze-dried vegetables and those you dry yourself do not.

HEAT DRYING VEGETABLES

For best results, all vegetables should be either blanched, steamed, dipped, or cooked. It's not absolutely necessary to take one of these steps in preparation for drying, but they help the appearance and flavor. Precooking does remove a bit of the food value, but precooked foods rehydrate quickly without heat and then only have to be warmed up. This is a definite advantage at altitude.

The pieces of the vegetables to be dried should be small and uniform—about the size of vegetables in a 10-ounce package of frozen mixed vegetables. Try to size them no bigger than ¼-inch thick whether sliced, diced, or whole.

Vegetables should be uniform in size because the smaller pieces will usually dry first. And if you leave them in the dehydrator too long, they will tend to overdry, or even burn.

To Blanch: Dip the cut vegetables in boiling water for 1 minute.

To Steam: Put the cut vegetables over steaming (full boil) water for 2 minutes.

To Dip (Brine): This is the oldest preparation, dating back centuries. Simply dip the vegetables in a brine solution for from 1 to 2 minutes. The brines should be enough to float an egg (½ cup of salt dissolved per quart of water). Hot brine at 1 minute works well.

To Dip (Natural Solutions): These are easy to use and provide excellent results. Use lemon, grapefruit, lime, pineapple juice either full strength or diluted up to 3 parts water to 1 part of juice. You can also use lemonade or a sweetened powder mix in these flavors. Frozen lemonade works well. Dip from 2 to 4 minutes, depending on the strength of the dip.

To Dip (Chemical Solutions): These solutions are often used commercially.

1. Use a solution of 1 tablespoon of *sodium bisulfite* to a gallon of water. Be certain to get *bisulFITE*, which is available at a make-your-own-wine shop. This chemical is used in wine making to preserve wine's color.
2. A solution of 1 tablespoon of *erythorbic acid* as above.
3. A solution of 1 tablespoon of *ascorbic acid* (Vitamin C) as above.

The above dipping times work well. If dipped longer, the vegetables take longer to dry. After blanching, steaming, dipping, or cooking, place the vegetables on a tray or screen; spread one layer deep and dry at 130°F. When dry, they are hard, like pebbles. Some, such as string beans, are like thin pieces of wire. If the vegetables turn brown, they have been in the dryer too long, or else the dryer is too hot.

Leafy vegetables such as cabbage or lettuce can be cut into strips about ½-inch wide and dried in small stacks of 3 or 4 strips. Leafy vegetables rehydrate in wilted form. The only vegetables that do not need to be blanched, steamed, cooked, or dipped, are tomatoes, mushrooms, onions, and garlic.

That's all there is to it. Size, dice, or slice the vegetables to about ¼-inch maximum, with the exception of yams, which should be as thin as possible.

DRYING FROZEN VEGETABLES

All commercially frozen vegetables have been prepared (blanched, steamed, or dipped) before freezing. These can simply be put on a tray or screen and then dried. They dry easily and well, and are often the least expensive and most convenient way of drying vegetables.

If you have never dried food before, you might start by buying a package of frozen mixed vegetables and drying them. After they are dry, take ½ cup of the dried vegetables and put them in 1 cup of water. Bring the water to a boil, and let it boil for 1 minute. Remove them from the heat (still covered), and let them sit for 15 minutes. Salt and eat.

You can add to this until you have a stew. Or you can just let the vegetables sit in the water without heat and let them rehydrate. Without heat, allow several hours for rehydration.

BEANS (KIDNEY, PINTO, SOY, LIMA, BLACKEYED PEAS, ETC.)

Beans are best for light-pack foods if they are fully cooked before they are dried. Cook the beans as you would normally. When they are fully cooked, wash them in cool water and heat dry them.

Smaller beans dry better than large ones. Small kidney beans will dry in their kidney shape. Large ones spread open as they dry. Canned beans dry easily. If you are going to dry these, use those canned in sugar, salt, and water only. Wash them off and dry them.

REFRIED BEANS

Take a can of refried beans, or make your own. Spread the beans on a tray, about ¼-inch thick and dry them. When they are dry, run them through the blender, and then package. Half a cup of ground, dried, refried beans needs about ¾ cup of water.

These rehydrate in an hour or so by cold soaking and don't need heat, except to warm them up. When rehydrated, they can be fried or used in any manner. They are also edible cold.

BEAN BALLS

Roll refried beans into small tight balls about ½ inch in diameter. Then roll the balls in flour and dry them.

These can be used in place of meatballs. For cooking, 2 ounces of dried bean balls require 3 ounces of water.

Put them in the hot water as late as possible. If they are boiled too long, they become mush.

BEAN SALAD

Make one, let it marinate. Then wash the beans and dry them. By cold soaking, they rehydrate in an hour. And the beans retain the marinade taste. You can also buy bean salads, wash, and then dry them.

A LARDER OF PREPARED BEANS
(SEE ALSO SATURATING DRIED FOODS.)

As a larder for trail use, beans are one of the easiest foods to prepare. Fully cook the beans and then dry them.

1. *Saturated in beef bouillon.* Usually use red or kidney beans. These can be used in "beef & beans," "chili & beans," and in stews, or by themselves with a little salt added.

2. *Saturated in brown sugar.* Put 1 pound of brown sugar in a quart or so of water and simmer this until the sugar is dissolved. Use this liquid to saturate the beans, adding more water only if necessary. If you add water, it's best to add brown sugar too.

3. *Cooked with salt only.* These beans are used in highly spiced gravies.

4. *Cooked with salt, pepper, onion, garlic, and oregano.* This is a "basic bean" and can be used with just about any dish or eaten as is.

5. *Saturated in a combination of dried onion soup and a canned taco or any chili mix.* These are used in a quick-and-good chili and bean dish, or they can be eaten as they are. Here are some preparation options:

Saturated small white (Navy) beans in brown sugar are a good sweet bean dish. They need little other than salt. Tomato can be added to the dish with a little mustard and some bacon. The result is a good Boston baked bean.

White beans can also be mixed in equal proportions with beans saturated in beef bouillon, and the result is an excellent bean dish.

Incidentally, as with any dried foods, these trail recipes can also be used at home. They are a great help to the time-pushed cook.

POTATOES

Dried potatoes are available in any grocery and all restaurant supply stores. They are available instant-mashed, sliced, shredded-hashed, and diced-hashed.

Dried instant-mashed potatoes can be ground to reduce bulk by one half. Instant-mashed can be made "lighter" in finished texture by adding 1 teaspoon of baking powder to 1 cup of ground. Do this before grinding so the ingredients are well mixed.

Ground instant-mashed can be used to fill the spaces between other ingredients such as vegetables in a stew mix. This adds food value and weight to the dish but no additional bulk.

Dried-ground, instant-mashed potatoes will absorb the necessary water without heat, thus helping you economize on heat. When rehydrated, they can be shaped into patties and fried.

Hash browns and sliced potatoes take several hours to absorb cold water. So if you plan to fry them for breakfast, soak them overnight.

HEAT DRYING POTATOES

Those you dry are going to taste a good deal better and cost much less than those you buy.

Slice the potatoes thin, about ⅛ inch, or cut them

into ¼-inch dices, then dip, blanch, or steam them for 1 or 2 minutes and dry them at 130°F.

If drying fully cooked potatoes, don't dip, blanch, or steam them. Just slice or dice them and dry at 130°F.

Dried potatoes may turn slightly brown in spots. This disappears when they rehydrate. It's a sign that they were in the dryer a bit too long, or the temperature was a bit too high.

To make instant-mashed, grind fully cooked and dried potatoes to a flour. The skins can be left on the potatoes. They give slightly more food value and a more pronounced taste.

Fully cooked, dried, and ground potatoes can be added to purchased instant-mashed. This gives a better tasting instant-mashed potato than when the purchased ones are used alone.

Frozen potatoes sold in the grocery can easily be dried. They are already dipped, blanched, or steamed. So simply put them on trays or screens and dry them. Frozen french fries can be dried in the same way. These will absorb the necessary water without heat and can be fried in a little grease.

Yams and sweet potatoes are available commercially dried. But you can dry them at home quickly and at much reduced cost. They are best dried after cooking. Yams must be sliced very thin, almost into flakes for proper drying. Sweet potatoes are the most useful and should be treated as normal white potatoes, as described in preceding paragraphs.

If yams or sweet potatoes are ground after drying, you can add raisins and brown sugar to the mix for an interesting and good tasting dish.

FRUITS

There are three basic types of lightweight fruits. Sun-dried and freeze-dried fruits are available commercially. And you can dry your own.

All fruits will dry (even as all vegetables will dry), and the variety available may seem endless.

The standard sun-dried fruits available in the grocery are usually apples (sliced, diced, and ready for sauce), apricots, dates, plums (prunes), figs, raisins and currants, pears, peaches, and mixtures. Delicatessens and health food stores will often have cherries, bananas, pineapples, and others.

Freeze-dried fruits are excellent for trail use. They may require more soaking time than the instructions call for. In taste and texture, they are often closer to canned fruit than fresh. And the freeze-drying process does not reduce their bulk as much as sun or oven drying.

If you are going to use commercially prepared "freeze-dried" compotes (mixtures of fruit and syrup), you should read the labels. There are many sold that do not have freeze-dried fruits; in this case, only the flavoring, and, sometimes, only a part of the flavoring is freeze-dried.

It normally takes from 5 to 6 pounds of raw fruit to make 1 pound sun-dried. These are the fruits normally sold in the store, and they have been reduced to around 28 percent moisture. This leaves them moist enough to eat without rehydration but dry enough to last.

DRYING "DRIED" FRUIT

You can take commercial, sun-dried fruits and dry them further. Just cut them into ½ inch or so pieces, and put them in the oven or dehydrator at 130°F. This reduces their bulk and weight by about one fourth. They will rehydrate in an hour or so simply by soaking. Applying heat will cut the rehydration time down to 10 or 15 minutes.

If you find the sun-dried fruits a little difficult to cut, rub a thin coat of flour onto the knife or scissors.

DRYING FRESH FRUITS IN AN OVEN OR DEHYDRATOR

Whether it's acerola, avocados, blueberries, strawberries or youngberries, all fruits will dry. And the same techniques are used for all of them.

Use fresh, ripe fruit, removing any blemishes. Discard or eat fruits with any blemishes, but don't dry them. Cut the larger fruits into slices about ¼- to ½-inch thick or into dices up to ½-inch square. Larger pieces can be used, but they take more time to dry. If you are going to use larger fruits (without slicing), pit them or core them and put them cut side up on the trays.

Very juicy fruits dry best when laid on a plastic film. After they are partially dry, remove them from the film. Also, you can cut the drying time of juicy fruits by blotting them to absorb some of the moisture before drying.

Fruits can be dried just as they are, but the results are better when you use a dipping solution. Any of the dipping solutions and dipping times are described earlier on pages 41–42.

Sometimes it's simplest to just use a strong lemonade and later add more water. You can then drink the lemonade, which goes well with gin or vodka.

If nothing else is available, use fruit saver, which is a grocery store item used in home freezing. With this use ½ cup per 2 quarts of water and dip for 3 to 4 minutes.

Once the fruit is dipped, spread it on the dehydrator, or oven shelves, and dry it at 130°F.

Some fruits, such as cranberries or plums, have thick outer skins. These should be blanched (dipped briefly in boiling water) to crack the skins so they will dry in a reasonable length of time.

Pineapples and cantaloupe are delightful and rewarding fruits to dry. Trim them and slice into ½-inch thick or thinner slices. Dip them and lay them on a plastic film for the first part of their drying. After they are partially dry, remove them from the plastic film and finish drying them on the racks.

If using frozen fruits from the store, just cut them to size and dry them. They have already been dipped and are ready for drying as they are.

Frozen blueberries dry quickly and are a rewarding dried fruit.

Avocados are a fruit (not a vegetable) that dries well. They are excellent for light packing. They should be sliced in slices ¼-inch thick for best drying.

Another interesting and pleasant way to dry fruit is to have baked apples for dinner. Bake an additional 6 to 12, and after they are baked, continue to dry them—including the skins. After drying, smaller apples can be fitted into larger ones.

These baked apples for drying should not have anything in the core, except sugar and spices.

USE OF DRIED FRUITS

These can be used as a snack—after rehydration if they are oven- or dehydrator-dried, before rehydration if they are sun-dried. You can make fruit soups or use with oatmeal, cornmeal, or any breakfast cereal, or with eggs, or as a compote, or in bannocks and pemmican.

If using in such dishes as oatmeal or bannock, it's most convenient to run the dried fruits through a grinder or blender and reduce them to small pieces. These smaller pieces rehydrate faster than larger pieces, and "pace" their rehydration more closely to the cooking of the dish.

FRUIT SOUPS

Fruit soups are traditional Colonial American dishes which are served in most European countries. They are good hot or cold. They are made with mixtures of ground dried fruits, sweetening, spices, and cornstarch to thicken. To quickly rehydrate and to make the cornstarch emulsify (thicken), these must be cooked before eating.

If you want to make a fruit soup that doesn't have to be cooked, substitute Sodium Alginate (see Thickeners section) for the cornstarch. (See also the fruit soups section [pp. 97–98] in Part III of this book.)

JAM

1 oz oven-dried or freeze-dried fruit,
   ground well
1 oz sugar

Grind or mix together well. Add 2 ounces of water
(¼ cup) and let soak until rehydrated. Heat helps make this
more like jams for home use. This is an excellent spread hot
or cold.

FRUIT LEATHERS

These thin sheets of dried puree are available in stores
or you can make your own. (Also see other references to
leathers in the book.)

To make them, simply prepare the fruit and puree it.
That is, mix it with a little water and run it through a blender
until it has the consistency of tomato sauce. Pour this on a
tray that has plastic film covering it. And dry.

You can add sugar or syrup, or well-ground nuts, and
mix the fruit flavors.

Tomato leathers can be made right from a can of
tomato sauce. But for better results, cook the tomatoes and
then puree them. If fruit leathers are chopped very small, they
make good additions to foods. Other than that, they are
usually used as snacks.

Caution: You can dry fruits on Teflon, wood, cheesecloth, fiberglass, nylon, plastic wrap, etc. But do NOT dry them
directly on metal because metal may give them a taste.

GRAINS, CEREALS, NUTS, AND SEEDS

All grains (barley, corn, millet, oats, rice, and wheat)
must be cooked in some manner to be digestible. Often, as
with popcorn, this means only a very brief application of heat.

Barley, millet, and wheat should be fully cooked and
then dried for trail use. They require a long cooking time, and
it's best to use the heat source you have at home.

Once cooked and dried, these grains can be used in the same ways as cooked and dried rice. (See upcoming pages.)

CORN

Corn is available freeze-dried or heat-dried, and can be dried at home easily and inexpensively. Just buy frozen, cut corn and dry it. When drying fresh corn, blanch it on the cob in order to set the milk. Then cut the kernels from the cob and dry them.

Corn dries quickly and should be watched and stirred occasionally, to keep it from browning.

If the hull is left intact on a kernel of corn, you'll find the corn difficult to digest, and thus you won't receive much food value from it. It may just pass right through you. Corn should be well chewed before being swallowed.

This same indigestibility or pass-through can be observed in uncooked grains.

Cornmeal and hominy grits work well with the One Minute Boil (OMB).

Cornmeal can be made by grinding dried corn into a flour or it can be purchased, but the commercial product is different from homemade flour.

Commercial cornmeal comes in three basic types: white, yellow, and masa harina. Masa harina is normally used in making corn tortillas and tastes slightly more like corn than the others. The yellow and white cornmeals were developed in Europe and the masa harina in Pre-Columbian America.

Cornmeal and hominy grits can be run through a grinder or blender to reduce their bulk slightly and to speed their cooking.

Some groceries and delicatessens stock Instant Polenta, which is a precooked maize (corn) flour that cooks quickly. This can also be ground to cut its bulk and cooking time.

Cornmeal and hominy grits are mixed 1 part meal to 4 parts water. If you grind them, add a little water because the

51

bulk is reduced by grinding. A good mix is 1 part ground meal to 4½ parts water.

To cook, mix the dried meal with a little water until it's a smooth paste and then add the balance of the water, stirring as you do. Give this a One Minute Boil (OMB) and let sit for 10 to 15 minutes. Or cook until done.

RICE

There are three basic types of rice: (1) raw (brown), (2) milled and polished (white), and (3) sweet glutinous (Mochi Gomi). There are many varieties of each. But for the purposes of this chapter, let's stick with the three basics above.

Brown and white rice are available in long or short grains. When long-grained rice cooks, the grains usually remain separate. When short-grained rice cooks, the grains cling together.

Sweet glutinous rice is used in making pastry and congee. It is not usually eaten as a simple rice dish.

Wild rice is not a rice. It is generally considered a separate type of grain. However, let's consider it rice for cooking purposes.

There are quick-cooking versions of all the above, excepting the sweet-glutinous, available in groceries or delicatessens. The quick-cooking and freeze-dried rices have more bulk than a rice that has been cooked and dried at home. The home-cooked and dried rice will also taste a good deal better.

Fully cooked rice dries very quickly. It will dry in some gas ovens overnight, with just the heat of the pilot light. If dried at 130°F, it dries in 2 to 4 hours.

After fully cooked rice is dried, it will rehydrate quickly without heat. And it's edible cold.

Rice can be cooked with seasonings (also see saturating foods), and then dried. When rehydrated, this is a seasoned rice.

There are three approaches to rice for light-pack cooking:

1. Completely cook and dry the rice at home, adding whatever seasonings when cooking. Or you can cook it plain and add the seasonings to the trail package. This second method will require more heat outdoors than the first because the seasonings have to be cooked. If fully cooked with seasonings, the rice can be rehydrated without heat and simply heated up. This is the most efficient method if you are going to be at higher altitudes.
2. Use quick-cooking or freeze-dried rice.
3. Carry regular, uncooked rice and try to cook it on the trail.

If rice is cooked at home with seasonings and then dried, the seasonings should dry quickly along with the rice. If the recipe calls for tomatoes, substitute tomato paste or tomato sauce. If onions are called for, use minced dry onions or flakes, or onion powder instead of fresh ones. Cut any other ingredients into the smallest pieces possible.

Do not use any fat, if possible. If you must use a fat, use lard or a good vegetable shortening, both having good shelf life without refrigeration.

COOKING BASIC RICE

There are many ways of cooking rice. One of the easiest is:

1   c rice (long-grain white rice)
1¾ c water
1   t salt

Cover and cook slowly over a very low heat, stirring once or twice, for 20 minutes at sea level, adding a minute for each 1,000 feet of altitude. If you use short-grain rice, add ½ cup of water. Brown rice takes about 40 minutes at sea level; add a minute for each 1,000 feet of altitude.

Spread evenly on trays and dry. It is dry when it acquires the same size and hardness it had before cooking.

To make spreading for drying easier, let the rice sit in a refrigerator overnight. It may then be necessary to run a little water over it to help separate the grains. The rice can also be sliced into "patties" ¼- to ½-inch thick and dried in these slices. After it's dried, it can be separated with a little pressure.

To rehydrate, add 1½ cups of water and let sit for an hour. Then warm it up. Or add the water for a One Minute Boil (OMB) and let sit 10 minutes. Or simply cook until done.

CONGEE

Congee is a sweet, glutinous rice gruel. It is a staple food of the poor in many areas as well as being considered a gourmet's delight.

Traditional recipes call for hours of cooking, but good results can be had by grinding the sweet rice to a flour and then cooking with a 2-minute boil and a sit-time of 15 minutes. You'll have to stir the mix fairly often to keep it from sticking to the bottom of the pot and burning.

For best results, grind the rice almost to a flour. The sweet rice flours, available commercially, don't work as well.

If sweet rice isn't available, short-grained or long-grained rice can be used. The results aren't as good, and you need twice the amount of rice.

In the following recipe for congee, the results are neutral in taste; flavorings should be added to it. All the cooking is done on the trail.

BASIC CONGEE

¼ c rice ground sweet (glutinous)
3 c water

Boil 2 minutes and let sit for 20 minutes. Or cook until done.

A number of recipes for congee appear in the recipe section, later in this book.

SUSHI

Sushi is a rice flavored with vinegar that is usually eaten with raw fish. It's good as it is or when used with vegetables. Sushi should be cooked and dried at home. On the trail, when cooking instant or minute rice, add the vinegar.

1 c short-grained white rice
3 T vinegar
½ t salt
1½ c water and cook as a basic rice

Dry the sushi and use it in any rice dish. It has a tart flavor due to the vinegar flavoring. It can be rehydrated and heated, and then eaten hot or cold with any normally eaten raw fish. Dip the fish in soy sauce. Of course, clean and fillet the fish. Don't eat the skin.

RICE AND TEA

Any instant, minute, freeze-dried, or cooked and dried rice can be cooked with tea. It's best to rehydrate cooked and dried basic rice in hot tea. You can also rehydrate the cooked and dried rice in cold tea and eat it cold, or heat the dish after rehydration.

OATS (ROLLED OATS, OATMEAL)

This is available in regular, minute, and instant varieties. Regular oatmeal can be ground to reduce its bulk and cooking time. It loses half its bulk and cooks in 5 minutes or less when ground.

One cup of unground oatmeal requires 2 cups of water to cook. However, the 1 cup when ground down into ½ cup still requires the 2 cups of water.

COMMERCIAL BREAKFAST CEREALS

Many cereals for outdoor use should be ground to reduce their bulk. Unground cereals can be added to the ground if you like the texture of the unground. Mixing the two reduces some bulk by filling the spaces between the unground with ground cereal.

When you eat dried cereals, you should also drink water or some other liquid. Cereals absorb a great deal of liquid quickly, and, without liquid, they can cause minor stomach pains.

Dry cereals that are normally eaten cold, such as Kellogg's Concentrate or Grape Nuts can, after grinding, be used as spreads. Just add water equal to 1½ times the volume of the cereal and let this sit awhile.

FOOD VALUE COMPARISON
(PER DRY OUNCE)

Name	Raw Bulk	Ground Bulk	Calories	Grams Protein	Liquid to add
Dry Gelatin*	¼ c	¼ c	98	24.5	?
Kellogg's Concentrate	⅓ c	⅙ c	106	11.3	⅓ c+
Fresh, Lean Beef (not dry)*	—	—	60	8.0	—
Life (Quaker)	1 c	¼ c	101	5.0	⅓ c+
Oatmeal	—		111	4.0	
Maltex	¼ c	¼ c	108	3.6	1 c
Bircher Muesli's*	⅓ c	¼ c	125*	3.0*	?
Farina (enriched)	⅙ c	⅙ c	106	3.0	1 c
Cream of Wheat	2½ T	2 T	100	3.0	1 c
Grape Nuts	¼ c	⅕ c	104	2.5	⅓ c
Hominy Grits	⅙ c	⅙ c	103	2.5	⅔ c
Corn Meal	¼ c	⅕ c	103	2.2	1 c

* *Bircher Muesli food values vary as the ingredients vary, about 20 percent.*

Bircher Muesli and Granola type foods can be made at home for about one-fourth the price of commercial products. Basically these are baked or roasted oatmeal with various additives. Here's how to make them:

> 4 c regular oatmeal
> 2 T honey or corn syrup
> ¼ c peanut or other vegetable oil
> ½ t salt
> ⅓ c water

Mix well together and spread thinly on trays. Bake for 2 hours at 225°F, or for 1½ hours at 250°F. Spread it again during the baking time. The "looser" the grains, the better.

When this is packaged, add such ingredients as raisins, nuts, and sugar.

There are many other cereals, of course. Check the labels and find their food values. There are also a number of excellent instant hot cereals with good food value. They are convenient on a trip, but most need some repackaging to reduce their bulk.

NUTS AND SEEDS

Nuts and seeds are high in calories, with most of the calories coming from fat. They can be eaten as snacks, ground into "butters," used as meat substitutes, blended with liquid, made into gruels or soups, and used in such foods as breads, bannocks, and fruit soups.

There are four factors in buying and carrying nuts or seeds: taste, availability, cost, and food value. No one can dispute your taste, and availability depends on locale. But it's good to know something about costs versus food values.

The accompanying table is based on dry and shelled 1-ounce portions. If a nut is roasted or fried, it will usually have a bit more food value, in the form of fat.

There are two kinds of "Pine" nuts. (See nos. 2 and 16, page 58.) The pignolia are gathered from a pine that grows throughout the Mediterranean area, although a few are grown in the United States. The pinon is native to the Southwestern United States, and the term "pinon nut" refers to several different types, with slightly different food values.

If you ask for "pine nuts," you are usually going to get pinon-type nuts. There is a real difference in food value between the two, and you should encounter a real difference in cost. However, the terms pignolia, pinon, and pine are often used interchangeably by commercial packers.

Type	Total Calories	Grams Protein	Grams Fat	Grams Carbo-hydrates
1. Soy "nuts" (not a nut, but often carried)	110	9.0	5.0	9.1
2. Pignolia (pine, also see No. 16)	156	8.8	13.4	3.3
3. Pumpkin (squash) seeds	157	8.2	13.2	4.2
4. Peanuts	160	7.4	13.5	5.3
5. Sunflower seeds	159	6.8	13.4	5.6
6. Butternuts	178	6.7	17.3	2.4
7. Walnuts (black, also see No. 13)	178	5.8	16.8	4.2
8. Pistachios	168	5.5	15.2	5.4
9. Beechnuts	161	5.5	14.2	5.8
10. Almonds	170	5.3	15.4	5.5
11. Sesame seeds	165	5.2	15.1	5.0
12. Cashews	159	4.9	13.0	8.3
13. Walnuts (English/Persian, also see No. 7)	185	4.2	18.1	4.5
14. Brazil nuts	185	4.1	19.0	3.1
15. Hickory nuts	191	3.7	19.5	3.6
16. Pinon (Pine, also see No. 2)	180	3.7	17.1	5.8
17. Filberts (hazelnuts)	180	3.6	17.7	4.7
18. Pilinuts	190	3.2	20.2	2.4
19. Pecans	195	2.6	20.2	4.1
20. Macadamia	196	2.2	20.3	4.5
21. Coconut (unsweetened)	188	2.0	18.4	6.5
22. Chestnuts*	107	1.9	1.2	22.2

* *Chestnuts are almost totally carbohydrates.*

It's also worth noting that the food value of the very *expensive* pignolia and the very *inexpensive* pumpkin seed is almost the same.

NUT BUTTERS

Peanut, cashew, sesame, and almond butters are widely available in cans or jars. These can be repackaged in plastic squeeze tubes or in plastic bags. If the oil has separated, be certain to mix it with the butter before repackaging.

Peanut butter is also available in a dried form. It's light to carry, but when water is added to it, it reduces (!) in bulk.

MAKING NUT BUTTERS

Take shelled and dried nuts (roasted or not, salted or not), and run them through a blender until they become a smooth butter. Usually you'll have to add a little oil at the beginning. Peanut oil or even bacon grease are recommended.

Add the nuts slowly as they grind into a butter. Package them in plastic squeeze tubes.

Nut butters made at home are usually dryer than those made commercially, and nuts can be mixed to achieve desired flavors.

RECIPE FOR PEANUT BUTTER:

2 slices bacon
2 c of roasted and salted Spanish peanuts

Fry the bacon until completely *crisp*. Put both the crisp bacon and the grease into the blender. Add the peanuts slowly until the entire mass is blended well. The result is an excellent peanut butter.

DRYING NUTS

To greatly reduce drying time required, dry nuts out of the shells. In the shell, nuts may require several days drying; out of the shells, they dry in 6 to 12 hours at 110°F.

It's easiest to put them out in the sun to dry and take them in at night. In a dryer, the best temperature is about 110°F, although nuts can be roasted at temperatures of 150°F to speed the drying time to several hours.

BANNOCK AND BREAD

The word *bannock* refers to a bread that is baked (or fried) on a hot, flat surface.

One pound of flour normally provides 1 pound of bannock or 1 pound of bread. This is the reason it's sometimes said that neither bannock nor bread belongs in a light pack. However, if you feel that bannock or bread is the staff of life, then you may want to pack it.

Old military manuals tell the baker to leave the bread in the bakery until it stales. When the bannock or bread is very dry, and even stale, it does seem to stick to your ribs better than when it is fresh.

Many armies throughout history used a measured amount of bannock or bread as a man's daily ration. This was often issued by the week and carried on a cord slung around the neck or in a very loose-woven cotton sack (bread bag).

Sometimes this was unleavened, simply "hardtack" as carried on sailing ships. If this daily ration was 1 pound, then it would have provided from 1200 to 1800 calories (depending on how it was made), and from 40 to 50 grams of protein.

There are three basic types of bannock: unleavened (those without any rising agent), leavened with baking soda or powder, and those leavened with yeast.

UNLEAVENED BANNOCK

This is the first "bread" made by man. It's simply flour and water baked on a hot flat surface. Unleavened bannocks made in this simple manner can last for years.

1 c flour
⅔ c water (enough to make a dough)

Mix the water slowly into the flour until it becomes a dough, firm enough to work with the hands. The dough should be a homogenous mass that holds together well.

Pull pieces from the dough, using a fork or spoon, and flatten them in a pan. Make them as thin as possible, only about ⅛-inch thick. (Or you can roll the dough into balls about the size of a small egg and then flatten them.)

Bake them on the surface of the pan for just a few

minutes on each side, until the edges start to curl and become slightly brown in spots. If the dough sticks to the pan, it is too moist. The remedy is to add flour. Even if too moist, the dough will eventually cook.

OATMEAL CAKES (SCONES)

The word bannock is Scottish in origin and originally referred to this type of bread.

1   c oatmeal
1½ c water (enough to make a dough)
1   t salt

Prepare and bake as you would unleavened bannock above.

LEAVENED BANNOCK (WITH BAKING POWDER OR BAKING SODA)

The leavening agent, baking powder or baking soda, gives off a gas as the dough bakes. The gas is "caught" in little pockets by the dough, causing the bread or bannock to rise. Thus it is leavened (lightened).

All leavened bannocks can be cooked with the lid on the pan. This makes for a small oven and shortens the cooking time. Leavened bannocks are generally thicker before baking than unleavened bannocks.

1   c flour
⅓ c water (enough to make a dough)
1   t baking powder or baking soda
½ t salt (optional)

Mix the ingredients together well. Add the water slowly to make a dough. Shape the dough into pieces about ¼-inch thick. You can speed up the cooking by forming a hole in the center.

Bake on the surface of the pan until the pieces are brown on each side. They get thicker and "lighter" as they bake.

LEAVENED BANNOCK (WITH YEAST)

These are the best tasting of all the bannocks. Yeasts are tiny, one-celled plants that "live on" sugar and starch. If sugar is also put into the water, the yeasts grow faster. They produce carbon dioxide gas, which makes the dough rise.

When making yeast breads at home, you must knead the dough and leave it for a time to rise (proof). This dough is then usually punched down to remove the gas that made it rise. Then knead it again and leave to rise a second time before baking.

Bannocks made outdoors are only ¼- to ½-inch thick and don't require the kneading. No rising is necessary. They will rise well enough while slowly baking.

Dried yeast is usually used. Since the yeast is made up of "living organisms," too much heat can kill it. Dried yeast is usually put into warm water to develop. It forms a grey foam about ¼- to ½-inch thick when it is active and ready to use.

Dried yeast will rise in cool water. Although this takes a bit longer, the yeast will rise. Again, if the water is too hot, it can kill the yeast. The water should be just warm enough to let you feel the warmth with your finger. To make basic yeast bannock, use:

> 1   c flour
> ½   pkg dried yeast
> 1   t sugar
> ¼   t salt

When packaging, keep the yeast and sugar separate (each to its own package) from the other ingredients. Mix the yeast and sugar with ½ cup of water (as above) and wait until the yeast forms a fairly grey foam on the water. Then mix the yeast, sugar, and water into the flour and salt. Mix slowly and add water as necessary, making a dough.

Divide the dough into pieces about the size of large eggs and flatten them from ¼- to ½-inch in thickness. Forming a hole in the middles will speed the cooking.

If you like, the yeast dough can be left to sit in the pan for 10 minutes. It will rise slightly, and one side will be very flat.

Put these on a pan and bake them until they are brown on each side, usually from 5 to 10 minutes per side.

GENERAL NOTES ON BANNOCK AND BREAD

A butter taste can be obtained by using margarine, butter, or butter-flavored salt.

Baking powder or baking soda can be used. Soda has a taste; powder does not. They can also be used mixed together.

Cornmeal can be sprinkled on bannock. It helps keep the bannock from sticking to the pan.

Various fruits, nuts, and meats can be added to bannocks. If they are dried, they should be ground small so they rehydrate "in pace" with the bannock's cooking.

Up to ¼ cup of fruits and nuts can be added to 1 cup of flour.

When cooking bannock over a small stove, be sure the pan is shifted about every 5 seconds or so or the bannock will burn.

PREPARED GROCERY MIXES

Any prepared mix, corn bread, blueberry muffin, cake mixes, biscuit mixes, self-rising flours, or pancake mixes can be used to make bannock.

COMMERCIALLY PREPARED BANNOCKS AND BREADS

"Pilot's Biscuits," many packaged "crisps," and other forms of hardtack are available in groceries and delicatessens. Some are the same as those sold as special trail food, but the grocery items are often half the price.

Check the weight against the size of the package. Some are very well packed and baked. Others take more space than necessary for the product. Repacking often will not help these because they are made slightly thicker, sometimes simply to ensure a larger package on the grocery shelf.

On a short trip, a loaf of sourdough bread may be worth considering. I can hear the disapproving voices now, but if sourdough is divided into daily portions and allowed to stale a bit (or to be dried in the oven), it's a good bargain as far as weight is concerned. Bulk? It's a bad bargain for its bulk. But for a short trip, bulk isn't any overriding concern. (Incidentally, sourdough is excellent fried in bacon grease.)

PANCAKES

Pancakes are simply leavened bannocks with a bit more water added to them so they can be poured into a pan. They may also have a bit more leavening agent. The easiest are the prepared mixes. They are reasonably inexpensive, and most people are familiar with them.

Pancakes, once made, can be carried like bread and eaten cold, with spreads on them.

Lightly grease the pan before adding the pancake batter. Syrup is available in concentrated form in most groceries. Or use any gravy, including beef, on them. Butter or margarine and a little brown sugar are often enough.

Making pancakes on a small stove poses the same problem that making bannock does: The pan must be kept in gentle motion much of the time, or the pancakes can burn. If keeping the pan in motion is inconvenient, at least move it every 5 seconds or so, changing the hot spot.

The fritter is an interesting pancake. Rehydrate some apples or other fruit and add a good measure to the batter, 1 part fruit to 4 parts batter. Then fry.

PASTA

The Italian word for paste—*pasta*—has come to mean any product made of flour paste, whether Italian macaroni, North African Couscous, Swiss Spaetzle, or Japanese Somen. Pasta is also called alimentary paste.

Marco Polo, writing in the late thirteenth century, popularized pasta in the Western World. Although Marco Polo popularized pasta, formed flour paste is one of the oldest known man-made foods.

Sir Francis Drake carried "hollow pipes" (macaroni) on his third voyage (1577–1580) for the same reasons we use it.

> "There is a certain victual in the form of hollow pipes . . . which I furnished Sir Francis Drake on his last voyage . . . it is very durable . . . exceedingly light . . . saves much fuel . . . is fresh . . . serves instead of bread and meat . . . (and) may be made as delicate as you please by the addition of oil, butter, sugar and such like."
>
> Hugh Platt (1596)

While there are over a thousand different shapes of pasta, the shapes that are of concern to the light packer are either the straight pieces or the very small ones such as Acini di Pepe (Peppercorns), Orza (Barley), and Couscous (the size of peppercorns).

Spaghetti (Italian for "little strings") and macaroni (hollow pieces) are made of a smooth paste of flour and water. This paste is usually shaped and dried.

Noodles, flat pieces usually, have eggs added to the flour and water paste. Some Oriental noodles will have the words "Imitation Noodles" on the package. This only means that they do not have eggs added to the flour and water paste. In Oriental or Hebrew pasta, the word noodle refers to all shapes.

Italian spaghetti comes in a number of thicknesses, from the very fine, almost as fine as a horse hair, to the oversized with a hole down the center called Spaghettoni. Orza is rice sized. Acini di Pepe and Couscous are the size of peppercorns. These last three weigh seven ounces per cup.

The thinnest Italian spaghetti available is called

Capelliani. In order of increasing size, they are called Fedelini, Vermicelli, Spaghettini, Spaghetti, and Spaghettoni.

The thinner the pasta, the faster it cooks and the less heat needed.

The thinnest Italian variety generally available is Vermicelli, which is also called Spaghetti No. 2.

Japanese "Somen" (very thin noodles) are thinner than Vermicelli and fall somewhere between Capelliani and Fedelini. Hebrew noodles are usually thinner than Vermicelli and about the thickness of Fedelini.

Pastas come in flavors. The easiest to find are vegetable flavors such as spinach. And they are made from different wheat flours. Italian pastas are usually made of the hard portions of Duram wheat. Oriental and Hebrew pastas are of softer wheats.

Oriental pastas are made of buckwheat (soba) or white (udon) wheat flour.

There are some quick-cooking macaroni on the market. These are the same as the regular types except that the walls are thinner. They do not save heat when using the One Minute Boil (OMB), but they require less sit-time.

There are also "Saimen" and "Ramen" noodles available that are partially cooked and dried. These are used in quick-cooking pasta soups.

Noodles come in many widths. The wider types are more difficult to use in a small pan because they stick together a great deal. Although even when stuck together, noodles are still edible.

The most convenient Italian noodle width is the Fettuccine (about ¼-inch wide) or the Fettuccelle (about ³⁄₁₆-inch wide). The smaller sizes, Trenette and Trenettine (about ⅛-inch wide), are not widely distributed.

Oriental noodles are often less than ⅛-inch wide. Sometimes they are almost square in cross section. They should be tried as they make a pleasant change of pace.

FREEZE-DRIED PASTA

Freeze-dried, cooked pasta appears only in a limited number of prepared freeze-dried dishes. The freeze-dried cooked pasta will turn to mush rather quickly. In cooking these dishes, you may find the meat is still crunchy when the pasta has turned to mush. To solve this problem, you should remove the meat and slice it as thin as possible before cooking. Then the meat might rehydrate almost as quickly as the pasta.

In other commercial packs, the pasta is common dried pasta, and the sauce—or part of it—is freeze-dried.

MAKING DRIED PASTA AT HOME

Pasta made at home is excellent.

> 1   c flour (bread flour if possible,
>   all-purpose if necessary)
> 1   egg
> ½   t salt
> 1   t oil
> 3   T water

Combine the egg, salt, oil, and water and blend them together well. Work them into the flour (adding a little water if necessary) until the flour is a firm dough. Knead the dough well and let it stand for 30 minutes or so.

Then roll and stretch the dough on a floured board, adding flour as needed, until the dough is almost transparent. Get the dough as thin as you can.

Hang the dough over cloth or a plastic wrap for about 20 minutes.

Lay the dough on the floured board, and sprinkle a light covering of flour over the dough.

Roll the dough up, like a jelly roll, and slice it in thin strips with a very sharp knife.

Unroll these thin strips and hang them up to dry if the kitchen is warm. Otherwise, hang them in your oven with just the pilot-light heat or in the dehydrator at the lowest possible heat.

When the dough is dry, treat as any dried pasta, *except* these will cook faster.

COOKING PASTA USING MINIMUM HEAT

Pasta works well with the One Minute Boil (OMB). While you may normally use great amounts of water at home and then drain the water and rinse the pasta, it is not necessary to do this. The more water you use, the more fuel you need to heat it.

Undrained and unrinsed pasta will have a slightly different, more concentrated, taste than those that are drained and rinsed. The difference in taste is due to the retained food value, which, if you pour excess water off, you simply "pour away."

Dry pasta will absorb, without becoming too mushy, 2½ ounces of water for each 1 ounce of dried pasta. If you are using a 7-inch pan, break the pasta into 4- to 6-inch pieces.

6 oz dried pasta
2 c water
½ t salt

Bring the water to a boil. Add the pasta a little at a time to keep it from sticking together. You may have to stir once or twice while doing this. Keep the water at a boil and stir gently for 1 minute. After a final stirring, cover the pan and wait for 2 or 5 seconds, no longer, and remove the pan from the heat and let sit.

The sit-time depends on how long the pasta is normally supposed to cook. If the size you are using (Vermicelli for instance) requires 7 minutes to cook, then the sit-time is the full 7 minutes. For Somen, the sit-time is 3 or 4 minutes. Cooking time is usually on the package of pasta that you buy.

When you use 2 cups of water to 6 ounces of dried pasta, there will usually be a little water left at the end of the sit-time. This liquid is used by the sauce if you put sauce in the water at the beginning, or it will be absorbed by the pasta in a few minutes. If it is absorbed, the pasta will be a little softer.

If you like your pasta "al dente" (a little bite to the teeth), then use 1¾ cups of water instead of 2 cups.

MAKING INSTANT PASTA AT HOME

Completely cook the pasta at home. Then dry it. Hang it (if spaghetti or noodles) from the racks of your oven or from dowels in the dehydrator. If the cooked pasta is macaroni, spread it on trays.

Dry at a fairly low temperature, 110 to 120°F. If at 130°F, check your drying pasta after 30 or 40 minutes, and spread it again.

The fully cooked and dried pasta will rehydrate without the use of heat. Once rehydrated, it is ready to eat cold. Or to heat it up, put a little water in your pan, add the rehydrated pasta, cover the pan, and heat.

This instant pasta can also be dropped into boiling water and let sit. No boiling time is needed, and the pasta takes 10 minutes to heat and rehydrate. If rehydrated in cold water, it will take 2 or 3 hours (see page 93).

COUSCOUS, FARFEL, SPAETZLE, ETC.

These are various names for other flour-paste products. They are often in the form of small pellets, available in groceries and delicatessens. They are used as dumpling (Spaetzle) or used in the same manner that rice is used.

SAUCES AND GRAVIES

Pasta can carry and enhance a wide range of flavors. Any sauce or gravy can be used with pasta. You can make a favorite sauce and then dry it to produce leather. When dried and ground, it can be rehydrated with the cooking pasta, or rehydrated before you rehydrate the pasta. Then pour it over the pasta.

Pasta is excellent with just salt, fresh pepper, and butter or margarine.

Any grocery sauce or gravy can be used on pasta. If the sauce or gravy needs heat, use the stove while the pasta is sitting. Some dried sauces call for milk. Instant milk can be added, or you can leave it out.

Other sauces and gravies call for the addition of tomato sauce. Tomato crystals can be used. Instant tomato soup is excellent here. Or the tomato can be left out. If it's left out, the taste is different, perhaps better. Tomato (pasta) sauce is usually very heavy in tomato taste, masking the taste of the pasta.

Cheese is traditionally used on many pasta dishes. Two sharp cheeses, Romano and Parmesan, are usually used. They are sometimes mixed together. Sharp dried blue or Roquefort cheeses that come as dried salad dressing or dried cheese dip are good, if used very lightly. The cheese in macaroni and cheese is usually a cheddar or sometimes a bland white cheese. A little dried blue or Roquefort, added to the other cheese, will give a pleasant, sharp taste to the dish.

A number of grocery items contain pasta and a dried sauce. Often these, including macaroni and cheese, require baking. But they can be handled quite well on a small stove.

Mix the sauce with water. If there are no instructions on the package, try about ½ cup of water but add a little only if it's needed. When it is well mixed, bring it to the boiling point, stirring once or twice as needed. As soon as the sauce begins to boil, take it off the stove and let it sit, covered, while you fix the pasta.

After the pasta is prepared, pour the sauce over it and mix well. Apply heat for just a short period of time, 5 or 6 seconds, if you think it necessary, and let it sit for another few minutes.

Some dried sauces have soda in them. These will swell when blended with cold water, so must be allowed enough room for them to "rise."

PASTA IN BRODA (PASTA SOUPS)

Pasta can be added to any broth, alone or with any combination of vegetables and meat. This makes a good soup.

Oriental pasta soups, Saimen and Ramen are easily available at most groceries, and at all Oriental delicatessens. They are made with precooked and dried Oriental noodles and a broth.

These quick-cooking versions are usually sold in 3-ounce packages. They take only 3 minutes of sit-time after being brought to a short boil. They are one of the fastest ways to a hot meal.

The least expensive Oriental versions are simply broth (shrimp, fish, chicken, beef, pork, etc.) and noodles. They become slightly more expensive, as the variety of ingredients increases.

Almost any dried vegetable or meat can be added. Just add what you like. Either rehydrate these additions before cooking or put them in the water when you start, for the noodles cook very quickly.

The 3-ounce packages are bulky. You can make good noodle soups by using a broth (chicken or beef is easy to find) and adding straight pieces of Somen or other Oriental noodles to it.

Cold pastas—soups or just cold pasta—are also popular in the Orient. Most are served only in hot weather. Mori Soba is cooked and then cooled. This is simply Oriental buckwheat noodles (soba) which are dipped in sweetened soy sauce as you eat them. Hiyamugi is the same, but, in this case, the noodles are made of white flour (udon), and the soy sauce is unsweetened.

Proper serving includes ice cubes. Unfortunately, rarely available on the trail in hot weather.

BEVERAGES

Almost all the items listed here are in dry, powdered form. To mix properly with liquid:

1. Put the dry ingredients in a little water in a container.
2. Mix well, adding more water if necessary, until you have a smooth paste.
3. Add the remaining water slowly, mixing as you do.
4. Most finished drinks will be better if allowed to sit for a few minutes before drinking.

MILK AND MILK SUBSTITUTES

This comes in many types of packages and under many brand names. Some forms are almost a powder. Others are in tiny pellets. Whatever the advertisements say, or however bright and big the package, these are basically the same, with only slight variations.

1. Whatever brand you buy, you should grind (blender) it until it is a powder. Some will require 3 cups to grind down to 1 cup, and others may require only 1½ cups. *After* grinding, 1 cup of instant nonfat dry milk will weigh close to 6 ounces, whatever the bulk before grinding.
2. Package this in ⅓ cup (2 ounce) portions, and blend 2 cups of water with it for an excellent trail-milk. This trail-milk will have approximately 102 calories and 10.2 grams of protein per cup, or 204 calories with 20.4 grams of protein per ⅓ cup (2 ounce) portion of ground instant nonfat milk.
3. There are some variations. For instance, there is a coconut instant drink mix (available at liquor stores and gourmet sections) that is mostly ground instant nonfat dry milk, but offers a very pleasant change.

INSTANT DRIED WHOLE MILK. This is excellent except that it is sometimes difficult to mix. Use small portions and mix carefully.

"BABY FOOD" AND SOY MILKS. SMA and Similac are available dried. These are light bulk and are suited to outdoor use. They are sweet tasting and are equal to, or superior to, whole cow's milk in the full range of food values. They can be treated just like regular whole milk. They do not have the same taste as cow's milk, so you probably should try one before you carry it.

NONDAIRY CREAMERS. From the grocery shelf, these taste like a good grade of cream. They have calories, but no protein to speak of. When mixed with ground nonfat dry milk, they add a rich creamlike taste. They are usually more difficult to mix in cold water than cow's milk. If adding them to ground nonfat instant milk, use 1 part nondairy creamer to 6 parts of ground nonfat instant milk, and grind them together.

DRIED BUTTERMILK. This is very sour. If you are going to drink this, first mix it with ground nonfat instant milk.

TEA

Carry the best you can afford and perhaps carry several flavors for variety. If you are going to carry tea bags, remember that you can get from 3 to 5 cups of good tea from each bag. If you are not going to make this much at a time, you can avoid excess bulk by carrying tea leaves.

To make a good cup of tea, bring the water to a boil and remove from the heat. Then put the tea into the water and let it "steep" until the tea is as strong as you like. If using tea leaves, put just a pinch or two into the cup.

A canteen of tea is pleasant. However, don't let the tea leaves sit in the water too long. The best way is to make it by the cup and pour the tea into the canteen.

Instant teas are good, especially when mixed or premixed with lemon.

Herb teas are not actually "tea" but are usually made

from dried flowers and herbs. They make an interesting change. Before you drink too much of any one, find out about it. Some teas are medicinal and are used for a variety of ailments from constipation to indigestion. An overdose can be unpleasant.

COFFEE

Carry the best you can afford. Often freeze-dried or regular instant coffees are carried. With these you can add sugar and cream to the dried coffee in the proportions you like.

Espresso can be flavored with cinnamon, allspice, nutmeg, etc. And with a lot of sugar used, you get a Turkish type of coffee.

The best coffee is made fresh from ground coffee. To get this, go to a gourmet store or a regular coffee-and-spice shop and buy a high grade of coffee. You'll pay more than you'd pay at the grocery, but you are getting a better coffee— one that goes farther per ounce. If you don't know coffees, stick to Java or one of the other heavy bodied coffees. Shop clerks often have good advice. Then have the coffee run twice through *the shop* grinder on the finest possible setting.

This results in a powder that yields a cup of *strong* coffee for 1 tablespoon of powder! A second cup can be made by adding ½ tablespoon to the grounds. If you like weaker coffee, just add extra hot water.

To make this coffee, you will need a funnel and paper filters. Buy a small plastic funnel that will fit your cup. Cut the spout and about ¾ inch of the funnel off. When the paper filter is put into this cut-down funnel, about ½ inch or so of the filter should be extending out of the bottom.

Put this into your cup, add 1 tablespoon of the twice-ground coffee, and slowly pour very hot water over it.

CHOCOLATE AND COCOA

Chocolate is available ready to use, sweetened, with milk in it, and even with some marshmallows. All you do is add hot water. This is the quickest and easiest way to do it. It's also the most expensive way.

You can make your own, saving weight, bulk, and money, by using powdered, unsweetened baker's chocolate or cocoa and sugar. Then just add dried milk and flavorings to your package.

> ½ t powdered unsweetened baker's chocolate or cocoa
> 2 t sugar (more or less to taste)

The above proportions are for 8 ounces of chocolate drink Pour boiling water over the mix slowly and stir well.

Ground (powdered) chocolate can be added to coffee (instant or regular) for a fine drink. A mixture of coffee, chocolate, and cinnamon is a favored drink in many parts of the world. This can be sweetened or not.

Carob powder can be used in the same manner. It tastes almost like chocolate.

FRUIT DRINKS

You can make your own or buy them in dried form at the store. When buying at the store, it is very important to read the labels. Expensive "trail" drinks are packaged that have almost exactly the same ingredients as inexpensive children's drinks from the grocery.

There are some excellent ones, even on the grocery shelf, where the main—or at least the second—ingredient is the fruit. Even if the label says "crystals," you should read the list of ingredients.

You are going to have to consider weight and bulk as well. For instance, 5 ounces of a freeze-dried trail-type orange juice makes up into 1 quart (32 ounces) of orange juice; 3¼ ounces of a "screwdriver" mix will make 1 quart; and 3.3 ounces of *sweetened* Kool Aid will make 1 quart.

Gelatin fruit drinks have a high protein and calorie

count. They taste fairly good, but are a bit heavy per ounce of juice.

Rose's Lime Juice is good. This is in concentrated and liquid form. One teaspoon will give 8 ounces of sweetened lime drink. This has, except for Shoffeitt's Dry Lemon Juice, the lightest weight and smallest carrying bulk of any commercial concentrated fruit drink.

FRUIT DRINKS YOU MAKE YOURSELF

These offer good flavor, and they are very refreshing.

You can take any fruit syrup or sweetened fruit nectar —whether purchased canned or made at home—and concentrate it by gentle simmering. (See Concentrating Liquids, page 19.) Eight ounces of syrup will usually condense into ½ to 1 ounce of thick liquid. To rehydrate, simply add 7 ounces of water and stir. These are carried in plastic baby bottles with the nipple reversed to make the seal watertight.

You can also make powdered-dried fruit drinks. Dry the fruit until it is hard, as discussed in the fruit section earlier in this book. Then grind the dried fruit into a flour. A mix of 1 part ground, dried fruit, and 1 part sugar works well; 1 or 2 tablespoons will give you 7 ounces of drink. However, this should be mixed with boiling water and then allowed to cool.

BOUILLONS AND SOUPS

These are often dissolved for hot drinks. But you can mix a packet of dried beef or chicken broth (bouillon) with cold water and have a cold consomme.

DIET DRINKS AND "INSTANT" BREAKFASTS

Diet drinks are often excellent outdoor drinks. They are intended to provide around 225 calories per 8-ounce glass as a "meal" for dieters. Most have around 10 grams of protein and 105 to 110 calories per 1 ounce, even if you mix with water.

You should do some label reading in this area. Several

"instant" breakfasts, which are basically the same as diet drinks, have less food value than some of the dieter's drinks

GRAIN BEVERAGES

Grain beverages, such as Postum, are useful as coffee substitutes, and you might find that you like them. If you have never tasted any, they are worth a try.

MALT BEVERAGES

Malt beverages like Ovaltine are good. These should usually be ground to reduce their bulk. They can be mixed with water without using milk. And they can be drunk hot or cold.

A plain malted milk is worthy of consideration. Mix a ground or powdered malt with ground instant nonfat dry milk. This also is good hot or cold.

You can also add Sodium Alginate (see Thickener section) to thicken the drink.

ROOT BEER, SARSAPARILLA, COLA, ETC.

These can be carried on the trail. Buy the concentrate and make a syrup according to package directions and carry the syrup. Usually it takes 1 teaspoon of syrup to make 6 ounces of noncarbonated drink.

There are many commercial extracts available, either in small or large amounts. Or you can get a few ounces of syrup from a "soda fountain." If you have a favorite soft drink, you can usually carry its syrup with you, as long as you don't mind having it noncarbonated.

In past times, root beer or sarsaparilla were about the only sweet drinks. They were often mixed with whiskey or rum.

RUM, VODKA, AND GIN

Rum and vodka are available in "concentrated" form. Rum is sold at 151 proof in most liquor stores. If you mix 1 ounce of this with 1 ounce (less just a drop or two) of water, you have a regular 80 proof rum.

"Vodka" is available (on prescription only) in 200 proof. Once opened, this drops to 180 proof in a very short while, just from exposure to the air. With this, you mix 1½ parts water to 1 part vodka.

You can add a few crushed juniper berries to this vodka, and after a few days it will taste like gin.

INSTANT "COCKTAIL" MIXES

These instant mixes are available at most liquor stores, and they are very concentrated. They run about ½ ounce of dried mix to a 6- or 8-ounce glass. They come in lime, tomato, orange, chocolate, and other flavors. As these are intended for use as regular cocktail mixes, they are flavored as such. They are good, but unique in taste. They have two things going for them: They are light and they have very small bulk. It's probably best to try them at home first.

DRIED SOUPS, GRAVIES, AND DRESSINGS

These all either have boiling water poured over them, or if they require cooking, they can be cooked until done or by the One Minute Boil (OMB).

Commercially manufactured dried soups and gravies are precisely made, whatever the quality. And the proportions of dried mix to water are usually accurate as given. Trying to thicken or increase the food value by cutting the water-to-add isn't advisable, especially with those that list salt as the first ingredient. Thickening or extending the food value is best done by adding ingredients.

There are a number of reasons to read the list of ingredients. As an example, tomato soup will often list tomatoes second or third on the list, in order of weight. These do not taste much like a good tomato soup, and are almost useless when substituted for tomatoes in chili or in stew.

The grocery will have about a dozen types such as pea, tomato, onion, mushroom, and vegetable. Some are instant soups that only require boiling water poured over them and a bit of stirring. Others will require more heat and some cooking time.

A good delicatessen will have many additional types such as clam chowder, lobster bisque, creme of almond, scotch broth, mock turtle, borscht, and senegalese.

An Oriental grocery will have clear soups (stock and mushrooms) and thick soups such as Ada Miso and Siro Miso (red and white soy bean soup mixes), in addition to some excellent fish soups.

Some of the dried soup mixes, especially when they have pasta in the package, are fairly bulky. The pasta can be crushed or removed and Orza, Acini di Pepe, or Couscous substituted with no loss of taste or flavor, but good reduction in bulk (see the pasta section earlier in this book).

Some of the packages will need repacking, and others can be used just as they are or reduced in bulk by putting a pinhole in them and exhausting the air. Then reseal the pinhole with tape, cut off the excess bag, and seal with tape.

Dried mixes should be blended with just a little water until they are a smooth paste. Then add the rest of the water slowly while stirring. Let the mix sit a few minutes before cooking.

The instant soups usually make 6 or 7 ounces of soup per ½ ounce package. There is good return on weight and bulk with them. They are also valuable as a quick appetizer while dinner or breakfast is being prepared.

Soups are considered breakfast in many parts of the world, and a good hot soup can make an excellent breakfast. If enough is made, it can be carried and eaten cold for lunch. Here you can add cooked and dried rice or potatoes, and let them rehydrate in the soup while you carry it.

DRIED SOUPS AND GRAVIES
AS A BASIS FOR STEWS

Starting with a dried soup or gravy, you can do a number of things by adding such precooked and dried or freeze-dried foods as rice, potatoes, vegetables, pasta, corn, barley, millet, lentils, and beans.

A number of suggestions are given in Part III under "Recipes and Field Techniques."

DRIED SALAD DRESSINGS

These come in small packets from the grocery. They usually call for the addition of oil and vinegar, although some need only water. They can all be used with just vinegar or just water.

Those in cheese flavors are very strong and quite good sprinkled lightly on pasta or potatoes.

MIXES FOR CHILI, TACOS, SLOPPY JOES

Only the best usually have tomato in them. Most of these mixes call for the addition of tomato paste or sauce. Tomato crystals or a good grade of tomato soup can be used. Use a soup brand that lists tomato first in the ingredients.

NOTES ON SOUPS, CHOWDERS, AND STEWS

You may choose to work only with grocery items, adding ingredients or using them as they are. Better dishes can be made at home, often as part of the regular dinner preparations, and then dried and carried.

A pure beef extract (sometimes called "Pocket Soup") can be made by following the techniques in the section on concentrating liquids, earlier in this book. Cut lean meat into small pieces and simmer them for 4 or 5 hours. Use 1 pound of meat to a quart or so of water. Keep the meat covered with water, and keep the pot covered, while simmering. After simmering, remove the meat from the broth and let the broth cool. When cool, remove all impurities (they cause mold), and all fat. Then concentrate the liquid. To turn the concentrate into powder, use cornstarch, as explained in the section on concentrating liquids.

Canned beef broth or bouillon can also be used, just concentrate and harden with cornstarch before grinding.

Pea soup can be made by grinding dry split peas into a flour. Unground split peas take hours to cook. Ground split peas take just a few minutes. Ingredients such as lentils and beans can be handled the same way.

These soups, made with legumes (peas, beans, and lentils), should be "bound." Cornstarch is a good and fast binder. The binding keeps the small particles of the legumes from separating from the broth and falling to the bottom of the dish.

Stews can be made at home, for home use, and the leftovers dried for trail use. If you are going to do this, it's important to use completely lean meat, and leave any fat or grease out of the stew.

When ready to dry a portion of the stew, separate the meat and vegetables, and dry the gravy as a leather. Cut the meat and vegetables into small pieces, about ¼-inch thick and dry them separately. Put the stew together again as you package it, adding 1 teaspoon of cornstarch for each cup and a half of gravy.

As with other dishes, it's best to weigh this before you dry it and again afterwards. The weight loss is the weight of the water—less 10 percent—used to rehydrate it.

CHEESE, EGGS, PUDDINGS, SUGARS AND CANDY, AND CONDIMENTS

CHEESE

In warm weather the best cheese for snacks is normally a hard cheddar, Swiss or Monterey. These should be cut into

1- or 2-ounce pieces, each piece wrapped in cheese cloth and then lightly dipped in paraffin. If you don't do this, be certain to wrap them, by the piece, tightly in plastic film. To inhibit the growth of mold, you can also wipe the cheese with vinegar, letting the vinegar dry before packaging.

This way you open only one portion at a time. If exposed to the air, the cheese will dry and after a few days start to mold. If it dries, you can use it in cooking or you can eat it. The mold should be cut off.

In cool weather you can carry almost any cheese, hard or soft, but the individual portions should still be well wrapped to avoid drying.

Cheese for cooking is often very hard. Grated Romano or Parmesan work well. These are available at most groceries.

Excellent "condensed" cheeses are packaged as dried salad dressings. These are usually a dried and powdered "blue" cheese. Use them very sparingly. They are good on pasta and in other cheese dishes to give a sharp, cheese flavor.

The spice section of the grocery will also have some dried and ground cheese that is sprinkled into dips or onto salads. These are good and give plenty of flavor with just a light sprinkle.

Packages of dried cheese sauce, enough to make about a cup of sauce, can be mixed in cold water and then heated. On the trail you can do this after the other dishes have been heated and are sitting.

Some of these cheese sauces have soda in them. These will rise to at least double their bulk if allowed to sit mixed in cold water.

EGGS

There are three types of dried eggs available: (1) commercial dried eggs, often used in school lunch programs or by bakers; (2) freeze-dried eggs; and (3) those you dry yourself.

The commercial dried eggs often have many additives. Because they change the taste, read the labels and buy those with the fewest additives. This type of dried egg is available in quart and gallon containers at restaurant supply stores for about one-tenth the cost per ounce of the small, two-egg packages.

Freeze-dried eggs are readily available and are often preferable to the above. They are expensive but easy to use, and they taste like eggs.

Eggs dried at home are also easy to use. They taste like real eggs, and they are the least expensive.

To rehydrate dried eggs, mix them well with the required amount of water. Then let them stand for 5 or 10 minutes. Cook them just as you cook fresh eggs.

DRYING EGGS AT HOME

Do a dozen or more at a time. Separate the whites and yolks. Whip the whites into a stiff meringue adding 1 teaspoon cream of tartar per dozen eggs. Meringue, when ready, is like a stiff whipped cream. Place this meringue on a plastic-film covered tray and dry it at 110 to 120°F. It dries in about an hour.

When dry, crush the whites into a powder and package them separately. Whip the yolks until they are smooth and pour this puree on a plastic-film covered tray. Dry as a leather. When it feels dry, crush it and grind it into a powder. Redry this powder on a tray. When finally dry, grind it again and package it separately.

To cook one egg, take 1 tablespoon of both the dried yolk and white and mix with 3 tablespoons of water. Let this sit 5 to 10 minutes until it becomes thick. These are used as fresh eggs, and they taste like fresh eggs.

DRYING HARD-BOILED EGG YOLKS

Cooked white of egg is one of the few things that will not dry properly. The yolks dry easily. Just cut them in half and dry. These rehydrate without heat and are useful in salads and other dishes.

INSTANT PUDDINGS

Instant puddings are available at almost all grocery stores. They do not require heat. Simply put them into a container with the liquid and shake them well. If the recipe on the package calls for milk, use ground powdered, instant non-fat milk. Put the ground milk into the dry package or add it just before you add the water. Add the necessary water and shake.

If you don't add the milk powder, the instant pudding will not jell.

Dietetic puddings are also available in powdered form. These are about one-fifth the weight of regular instant pudding and worth considering for this reason. They have fewer calories than regular instant puddings.

A "rennet" type pudding (Junket is good) can easily be made. One tablet will transform a couple of cups of milk into a pudding. In hot weather eat these within an hour or two. They tend to separate into "curds and whey."

SUGARS AND CANDY

Glucose is less sweet than cane or beet sugar. Fructose is slightly sweeter than cane or beet sugar. Both come from fruits, and glucose also comes from some vegetables, especially corn. Both are slightly easier to digest than cane or beet sugar.

Dextrose is a form of glucose, and is found naturally in fruits and certain vegetables and honey. It is easy to digest as it is the sugar already present in your blood. Dextrose is also called grape sugar (see page 128).

Honey is one of the best of all foods, as far as energy and quick digestion are concerned. Honey is twice the sweetness of cane or beet sugar, and nearly twice the weight. Honey comes in natural flavors, depending on where the bees gathered it. If it crystalizes, the crystals can be eaten, or an application of heat will dissolve them.

Maple sugar is much sweeter than cane or beet sugar and slightly heavier.

Brown sugar has an excellent taste, like molasses, and can be used where molasses is called for.

"Energy" bars (sometimes called "Space Food") are available at most sporting or backpacker stores, at health food stores, and often at the grocery. They rarely have more "energy" than any candy bar, often less. They usually cost more than other forms of candy.

The word pemmican is sometimes misused commercially to describe various types of candy or fruit bars. See the section on pemmican earlier.

An excellent "energy" bar can be easily made at home with a fair saving in cost.

CHOCOLATE AND NUT BAR

2 oz ground dried nuts
2 oz semisweet chocolate

Put the ground nuts in a container lined with plastic film. Melt the chocolate and pour it over the nuts. Let it harden.

If you want to add dried fruits you can, but remember that fruits have less calories than nuts. The food value of the bar above is from 152 to 170 calories (depending on the nuts used) with around 4 grams protein and 15 or so grams fat per ounce.

GORPS

The type of candy or sweet you carry is a matter of personal taste. Various items can be mixed into "gorps," such as small pieces of chocolate, raisins, and nuts. These can be eaten by the handful. The mixtures usually have a high calorie count, about 130 to 150 calories per ounce.

CONDIMENTS (SALT, PEPPER, MUSTARD, VINEGAR, ETC.)

There are several different types of salt, and they can have slightly different flavors. Salt can be ground to reduce its bulk and speed its dissolving.

Butter-flavored salt can be used for a slightly buttery taste. Sometimes this is sold under the name "popcorn salt."

Hickory-smoked salt has a strong wood-smoke taste and can be used to give a slight "bacon" taste to food. It's very strong in smoke flavor and should be used very sparingly. Otherwise it may spoil the dish.

There are also many seasoned salts on the market. If you use them at home, and like them, why not carry them?

Pepper is best when freshly ground. It loses flavor if exposed to air for a time. Pepper can be purchased in ⅛ ounce and even smaller portions at a restaurant supply store.

Mayonnaise, ketchup, and mustard are available in small plastic squeeze bags at restaurant supply houses. They carry and keep well.

Mustard is also available dry in the spice section of the grocery. Just mix it with water. But this is a very hot mustard, and should be tried at home first.

Jarred mustards, whether "baseball" mustard or a fancy Dijon, dry well. Just spread on a plastic-film covered tray and dry as a leather. Grind after dry and then package. Rather than dry a bit at a time, do a jar or two and keep it, taking what you need each trip. Jarred mustards are about 75% water before drying.

Vinegar can be condensed. Eight ounces (1 cup) can be reduced over heat to less than an ounce. (See also the section earlier on concentrating liquids.) This concentrate is very strong vinegar. Mix the concentrate with water at 7 to 1 and you'll have a vinegar rehydrated in normal strength.

The condensed vinegar can be dried by saturating rice or wheat kernels with it. (See Saturating foods.) These kernels can then be crushed or ground and used. Here the mix is 4 or 5 parts water to 1 part dried. This vinegar also takes an hour to rehydrate in cold water.

In the seventeenth century, strong vinegar was beaten in a mortar with blades of green wheat or rye and then rolled into small balls and sun-dried.

Note: If you are going to reduce or concentrate vinegar over heat, do it outdoors. The odor is strong, unpleasant, and longlasting.

BUTTER, MARGARINE, OILS, AND FATS

Oils and fats have the highest calorie count per ounce of all foods, and for this they belong in a light pack. When properly handled, they should stay sweet at least from 1 to 6 months.

Lard, vegetable fats (shortenings), and oils have 250 calories per ounce. Clarified butter has about 240, margarine about 205, and bacon grease about 200. The last three may have a few more or a few less calories depending on how they are made, and what goes into them.

BUTTER AND MARGARINE

Butter made at home or bought at a store is not clarified. Unclarified butter turns rancid in a short period of time. This may take only a day or so in hot weather.

Clarified butter (butter oil, dehydrated butter) will last a reasonably long time. Normally, it will last 4 or 5 days to 7 days without refrigeration even in hot weather. In cool or cold weather it can last months.

It's easiest to clarify butter 2 or 3 pounds at a time. Put the butter in the top of a double boiler and slowly heat it. Let it stay on the heat, very gentle heat, simmering lightly for ½ hour. Foam will rise to the top and sediment will fall to the bottom. Use these as kitchen butter.

Repeat the process with the "oil of butter" for another 20 minutes or so. Carefully remove any additional sediment or foam and package the "oil of butter."

Package it in sterilized plastic baby bottles, leaving an inch or so at the top. For longest trail-life, these should be kept in a freezer until carried.

Clarified butter has a very fine and delicate taste, very much like "trail butter." (See below.)

Butter is also available in cans. Once opened these must be treated as fresh, unclarified butter.

Some margarines are made entirely with vegetable oil and do not require refrigeration, either at home, at the grocery, or on the trail. In very hot weather, these should be used within 10 days. Once a large manufacturer kept cases of their all-vegetable margarine at a constant 70° for 2 months. Some turned rancid; some did not. There was no apparent explanation because all the margarine came from the same batch.

TRAIL BUTTER

This is a light tasting and good "butter." It will keep as long as, or longer than, vegetable margarines. It's made from any high quality vegetable shortening by adding a butter extract (spice section of a grocery) and salt.

Boil water in a clean pan. Pour the water out and put the vegetable shortening into the pan. Add a little butter extract (try 16 drops per pound) and ½ teaspoon of salt. Let the vegetable shortening melt and stir all together well.

Pour into a sterilized plastic baby bottle or plastic squeeze tube and seal, leaving an inch at the top. If you like your "butter" yellow, add 14 or 15 drops of yellow food coloring per pound while the butter is warm.

BUTTER (IMITATION) FLAVORED SALT

This gives a slight butter taste and should be used as a salt substitute. It's also called "popcorn salt."

LARD

Lard is a traditional frying and cooking grease. It accents the flavors of the food it's used with. Always use or carry the "no refrigeration needed" type. This is made to last for a considerable time without refrigeration.

BACON GREASE

Almost anyone over the age of 40 can recall seeing their mother keep bacon grease in a can in the cupboard for months, adding to it and taking from it as needed. Unfortunately, much bacon today is cured with a light combination of sugar, water, and some salt. Even so, this grease will last a good length of time. The grease from bacon that's fully salt cured should last about a month under normal outdoor conditions.

OIL AND VEGETABLE FATS

Oils, such as peanut, soy, olive, and corn will keep well even in hot weather. They should be kept as cool as possible and in a dark area. As with all foods, oils and fats should not be exposed to sunlight or excessive heat. They should stay sweet for almost any trip.

Vegetable fats are solidified oils and have the same attributes as the oils.

PART

III

RECIPES
AND
FIELD
TECHNIQUES

SALADS

Freeze-dried chicken and tuna salad are available. If you make your own salads, you can use any of the following for dressing:

1. Mayonnaise in small packets (See the section on condiments, earlier.)
2. Sour cream is available dried and mixes well with water.
3. Vinegar (See the condiments section, earlier.)
4. Any of the dried salad dressings available in the grocery (See the dried soups, gravies, and salad dressing section, earlier.)

Lettuce when dried has a different, more concentrated, flavor. It rehydrates limp with a trace of this concentrated taste. But it tastes good dry and broken up sprinkled over a salad.

If you are going to use a salad, other than freeze-dried, as a cold lunch, it should be put into water and rehydrated during the morning. These salads take from 1 to 3 hours to rehydrate in cold water.

AVOCADO SALAD

Avocados dry easily (See the fruit section, earlier.)

½ c dried avocado dices or slices
¼ c dried celery
½ t minced dried onions

Rehydrate in about 1 cup cool water. When rehydrated, pour off any excess water or use it in making the dressing. Put the dressing of your choice over it and eat. You can also mash it together and use it as a spread. Or you can add a touch of garlic and a pinch of chili before rehydration. After mashing it together, call it Guacamole.

BEAN SALAD

You can use any combination of cooked and dried beans, or as described in the section on vegetables earlier in this book. You can buy a jar of bean salad and dry it, or make your own and dry it. Rehydrate in 1 cup of water to ⅔ cup dried beans. The marinade taste will remain in the rehydrated beans.

CARROT SALAD

Shred fresh carrots (or use diced) and blanch for just 5 seconds, no longer, or steam them for 30 to 40 seconds. Dry them. If you use dried diced, you may want to grind them just slightly.

½ to 1 c dried carrots
¼ c raisins

Rehydrate in triple the volume of cool water. Pour off the remaining water and use any dressing you like. Mayonnaise is usually used. Mix well and eat.

CAULIFLOWER SALAD

Marinate fresh cauliflower (small flowerlets) in vinegar and dehydrate them.

½ to 1 c dried cauliflower
1 T dried celery

Rehydrate in 1 to 1½ cups of cool water. Pour off the remaining water and add mayonnaise or eat it as it is.

GARBANZO (CHICK PEA) SALAD

Fully cook the garbanzo beans and marinate them. Dry them. Rehydrate in double the volume of water. Add a dressing or eat as is.

MACARONI SALAD

Fully cook salad macaroni (tubes about ¼-inch long) and make your macaroni salad as you normally do—but do not use mayonnaise. Dry these ingredients. Rehydrate in double their volume of cool water. Add mayonnaise. Mix and eat.

If you don't have a special recipe for the ingredients of a macaroni salad, use cooked macaroni and dry it. Mix this dried macaroni with a few dried minced onions and a couple of dried egg yolks. Rehydrate and use mayonnaise as the dressing.

POTATO SALAD

> ½ c cooked dried and diced potatoes
> 2 or 3 dried hard-boiled egg yolks
> 1 t minced dried onion

Rehydrate in 1¼ cups of cool water. Use remaining water to make sour cream dressing, or pour off water and use mayonnaise. Salt.

VEGETABLE SALAD

Several forms of dried salad vegetables are available at restaurant supply stores. You can use these, rehydrate, and dress as you like. Or you can put together any combination of dried vegetables. (The contents of a frozen mixed vegetable package are good.) Rehydrate and use the dressing of your choice.

WALDORF SALAD

In its simplest form, this is a mixture of apples and walnuts with mayonnaise. Use heat-dried apples and partially ground walnuts.

> ½ c heat-dried apple dices
> ¼ c partially ground walnuts

Rehydrate and use mayonnaise.

SOUPS AND CHOWDERS

BEEF AND BARLEY SOUP NO. 1

Package the following together:

½ c cooked and dried barley
2 beef bouillon cubes or packets of
dried beef bouillon

To cook: Add 2 cups of water.

BEEF AND BARLEY SOUP NO. 2

¾ c barley (saturated in beef bouillon)

To cook: Add 2 cups of water.

BEEF AND BARLEY SOUP NO. 3

Add to above:

1 T dried minced onions
1 oz cooked and dried beef

To cook: Add 2 cups of water.

CHICKEN AND RICE

½ c cooked and dried rice, or minute rice
2 chicken bouillon cubes or packets of
dried chicken bouillon

To cook: Add 2 cups of water.

MINESTRONE

½ c dried vegetables
½ c flat noodles in 1 inch lengths
2 beef or chicken bouillon cubes
or packets of dried
1 t cornstarch
garlic, salt, and pepper

Run the vegetables through a blender and reduce their
bulk slightly before packaging. To cook: Add 2 cups of water.

CORN CHOWDER

½ c dried corn
½ c dried diced potatoes
¼ c ground instant mashed potatoes
1 T dried minced onion
1 package of tomato soup (or that part of a package that calls for 2 cups of water)
salt and pepper

Add 2 cups of water, mix well, One Minute Boil (OMB), and let sit for 15 to 20 minutes.

BEAN PORRIDGE

½ c dried and ground refried beans
½ c dried cooked beans
2 oz ground, dried, cooked meat
1 T cornmeal
1 t cornstarch
salt and pepper

Add 2 cups of water, stir well, OMB, and let sit 15 to 20 minutes.

SWEET POTATO CHOWDER

⅔ c cooked and dried sweet potatoes
2 T brown sugar
¼ c raisins
¼ c ground peanuts or 2 T peanut butter
2 t cornstarch
2 packets chicken broth or bouillon cubes
1 t cornstarch
¼ t nutmeg
¼ t cinnamon

Add 2 cups of water, stir well, OMB, and let sit 15 to 20 minutes. You can substitute dried squash or pumpkin for the sweet potatoes.

POTATO CHOWDER

        ¼ c dried diced potatoes
        ½ c ground instant mashed potatoes
        2 T dried onion
        2 packets beef or chicken broth or
              other broth option
           salt and pepper

Add 2 cups of water, stir, OMB, and let sit 15 to 20 minutes. You can use dried tomato soup in the above.

PEA SOUP

        ¼ c well ground (floured) dried peas
        1 T dried minced onion
        2 t cornstarch
           pinch or so of garlic powder
           salt and pepper

Mix with ½ cup of water until a smooth paste. Then add 1½ cups (or slightly more) of water, mixing as you do. OMB and let sit 15 to 20 minutes.

BEAN SOUPS

You can work in the same manner as pea soup, above, or use ground, dried refried beans. Or use completely cooked, dried, and ground beans. The best results are obtained using ground, dried refried beans. Instead of ¼ cup peas use ⅔ cup dried refries.

Bacon that you salt-cure yourself is good here. Slice the bacon very thin and boil it for a few minutes in a little water. Use this water and the bacon for the soup.

APRICOT SOUP

        3 oz heat-dried and ground apricots
        1 oz sugar (white or brown)
        1½ t cornstarch
        1 t dried and ground lemon peel, or
              ¼ t dry lemon juice

To cook: Add 2 cups or less of water.

PINEAPPLE AND APRICOT SOUP

Add 2 ounces of heat-dried and ground pineapple to the soup above.

APPLE AND PINEAPPLE SOUP

3   oz heat-dried and ground apples
1   oz heat-dried and ground pineapple
1   oz white sugar
1½ t cornstarch
¼   t cinnamon

To cook: Add 2 cups of water.

FRUIT "STEWS"

Cooked, dried, and ground chicken or turkey and rice can be added to the above. The cooked and dried rice will extend the dish, adding food value inexpensively. Half a cup of rice should be enough. No additional water is needed. (Also check various references to fruit soups, as noted in the Index.)

COMMERCIALLY DRIED SOUPS AND GRAVIES IN STEWS (also see page 78)

The following recipes are designed to be used with 2 cups of soup. If the package being used calls for more or less than 2 cups, change the proportions accordingly.

CLAM CHOWDER SOUP MIX

Add:

⅓ c cooked and dried diced potatoes
¼ c dried fresh or frozen peas (cooked),
    slightly ground

Rehydrate the potatoes and peas beforehand or put them in the water when you start to heat it. OMB and allow sit-time of 15 to 20 minutes.

CREAM OF CHICKEN SOUP MIX

Add:

½ c cooked and dried rice or ¾ c instant or
freeze-dried rice or add ½ c cooked and
dried diced potatoes
¼ c dried vegetables
½ to 1 oz cooked and dried chicken

Put into the water. OMB and allow a sit-time of 15 to
20 minutes.

MUSHROOM SOUP MIX (or HUNTER'S SAUCE)

Add:

½ c cooked and dried rice or ¾ c instant or
freeze-dried rice or ½ c cooked and dried
barley or 1 c cooked and dried potatoes
1 oz cooked and dried meat
¼ c dried vegetables

OMB and allow sit-time of 15 to 20 minutes.

OXTAIL SOUP MIX

Add:

½ to ¾ c cooked and dried barley

Let the barley rehydrate while the water is heating.
Blend the soup mix with cold water and add it to the boiling
water and barley. OMB and allow sit-time of 15 to 20 minutes.

PEA SOUP

Add:

½ to 1 c cooked and dried potatoes

OMB and allow sit-time of 15 to 20 minutes.

POTATO OR LEEK SOUP MIX

Rehydrate ½ cup dried corn and add it to the soup before removing the soup from the heat.

Add ⅕ ounce of dried bonita flakes (See the section on fish, page 37) to the water before heating, or add 1 ounce of ground and dried fish or shrimp.

Use 2 packets chicken broth in the water and add 1 ounce of cooked and dried chicken to the water before heating. One-half or one-fourth cup rehydrated peas are also good here.

Add any small fish—cleaned, skinned, and deboned.

SCOTCH BROTH SOUP MIX

This is the basis of an Irish Stew if you like. Add:

- ½ to ¾ c cooked dried diced potatoes
- ½ c dried cooked peas
- ¼ c dried celery

OMB and let sit 20 to 25 minutes, or reheat for best results.

SENGALEZ SOUP MIX

Sengalez soup has curry. So add:

- ½ c dried apples
- ½ c cooked and dried rice or instant or freeze-dried
- ¼ c raisins

Rehydrate the above and add it to the water when you start. Or put in the water to start and OMB with a sit-time of 15 to 20 minutes.

TURKEY GRAVY MIX

Bring the water to a boil and use any bread dressing. Put the dressing in the boiling water and stir well. Set this aside, make the gravy, and pour it over the dressing. Or mix all together for a good tasting mush. Or you can add:

¾ c cooked and dried sweet potatoes
¼ c dried celery
¼ c dried raisins
1 oz dried cashews or almonds
1 oz cooked, ground and dried turkey (optional)

Put the water into the pan and add the above. Then heat the water. OMB and stir in the gravy mix. Let sit 15 to 20 minutes.

VEGETABLE SOUP MIXES

Add pasta and make them "minestrones," or add rice.

WINE SAUCE MIXES

There are two easily available: Burgundy and white wine sauce. For chicken in wine sauce, you can use either. Then add as follows:

1 oz cooked and dried chicken
½ c cooked and dried rice or
½ c cooked and dried potatoes
¼ c dried peas

Put the above in the water and bring the water to a boil. OMB and let sit 15 minutes. Add the wine sauce and bring to a boil again for just a second. Cover and let sit for 5 to 10 minutes.

For beef and wine sauce, use the burgundy sauce mix and substitute 1 ounce cooked and dried beef for the chicken. Proceed as above.

BANNOCKS AND BREADS

Recipes are given here for packaging at home and cooking on the trail. For cooking method(s) see pages 59 to 63.

UNLEAVENED BANNOCKS

TORTILLAS (CORN)

1 c masa harina (page 51)
1 t salt

Add ⅔ cup of water, enough to make a dough.

TORTILLAS (WHEAT)

1 c white flour
1 t salt

Add ⅔ cup of water, enough to make a dough.

OATMEAL CAKES (SCONES) see page 61

POTATO SCONES

⅔ c instant mashed potatoes
⅓ c flour (white)

Add 2 or 3 tablespoons of grease and enough water to make a dough.

LEAVENED (BAKING POWDER OR BAKING SODA) BANNOCKS (page 61)

PLAIN, BASIC

1 c flour (white)
1 t baking soda or powder
½ t salt

Add enough water to make a dough.

POTATO BANNOCK

3 oz potato pancake mix
3 oz white flour
1 t baking powder or soda
salt

Add enough water to make a dough.

CORN BREAD

You can use a regular corn bread mix and instead of baking it in the oven, simply bake it in a pan. Or you can do this:

> ½ c corn meal
> 1 c white flour
> 1 T baking powder or soda
> ¼ t salt

Add enough water to make a dough.

HUSH PUPPIES

Add 1 tablespoon of dried minced onions and a bit of pepper to corn bread. Rehydrate the onions before using. Prepare as above, *except* Hush Puppies should be fried in grease!

Traditionally Hush Puppies are fried in deep grease, but they are equally good if the grease is only about an ⅛-inch deep. Turn them several times, cooking them on all sides.

HOECAKE AND JOHNNY CAKE

These are usually simply cornmeal, water, and salt with a rising agent.

> ½ c cornmeal
> 1 c water
> 1 t baking powder or baking soda
> ½ t salt

Mix well and let stand for 20 minutes.

LEAVENED (YEAST) BANNOCK (page 62)

CORN DISHES (also see pages 51–52)

CORNMEAL MUSH

> ½ c cornmeal or hominy grits
> ½ t salt

To cook add 2 cups of water. This can be eaten as is, or with sugar, syrup, or gravy—either hot or cold. Onions, fruits, and meats can be added.

FRIED CORNMEAL MUSH

Let cornmeal mush sit until it cools and it will "jell." Slice the "jelled" cornmeal in ½-inch slices, coat them with flour, and fry in grease. Serve as is or with butter, bacon grease, honey, etc.

SCRAPPLE

½ c cornmeal or hominy grits
¼ c whole wheat or white flour
¼ c cooked and dried meat, slightly ground
2 bouillon cubes or packets of dried bouillon (beef if beef is the meat; chicken if chicken)
1 pinch each of sage and marjoram
salt

Add 2½ cups of water and cook. Let sit until jelled and fry as fried cornmeal mush.

TAMAL EN CAZUEZ (CASSEROLE TAMALE)

A dish similar to this is eaten in Latin America.

½ c cornmeal
¼ c masa harina (Check Index references.) If you don't have masa harina, add ¼ c cornmeal
¼ c cooked and dried, slightly ground, beef
1 T dried minced onion
1 pinch of garlic powder
½ t dried oregano or marjoram
salt

Add 2½ cups of water and proceed as for scrapple.

Chili powder can be added, as can tomatoes and fruit. This is excellent eaten as a mush, hot or cold or fried.

SUCCOTASH

Succotash is a mixture of broad beans (limas), corn, and meat.

½ c dried sweet corn
½ c dried cooked limas
1 oz dried cooked and ground beef
salt and pepper

Add 1½ cups of water and some grease.

POPCORN

One ounce of unpopped popcorn makes over 3 cups of popped corn. Each cup of the popped corn has about 42 calories and 1.4 grams of protein, in addition to being an excellent snack.

Put a little oil in the bottom of your pan, it doesn't have to be much, but be sure the entire bottom of the pan is, at least, well greased. This adds calories and keeps the popcorn from sticking to the bottom and burning the pan. It's almost impossible to get the burned marks out of the pan.

Put 1 ounce of unpopped popcorn in the pan. Cover and hold it close to your heat source. Move the pan back and forth slowly but continuously, sliding the popcorn around inside.

Within a minute the corn should start to pop and should be all popped within another minute.

Salt and eat, or carry with you.

POTATOES (also see pages 45–46)

It's quite possible to package a "universal" potato mix and simply dive into it and use it for any mashed potato needs, whatever they are.

"UNIVERSAL" POTATO MIX

1   lb instant mashed potatoes
2   T minced dried onions
½   t garlic powder or 1 t flakes
2   T baking powder
1   t cornstarch
2   oz nonfat dry milk
4   packets dried beef bouillon
1   t salt

Grind them all together in the blender. This may get dull after a few days of it.

SCALLOPED POTATOES

These can be purchased already packaged in the grocery, or you can make your own.

1 c diced dried cooked potatoes
2 T ground instant nonfat milk
1 T dried minced onions
1 t cornstarch
salt and pepper

Add 1¾ cups of water and stir well. OMB and 15 to 20 minutes of sit-time or cook until done.

GERMAN POTATOES

There are many names for this and many versions of it.

1 c diced or sliced dried potatoes
1 T dried minced onion
2 dried eggs

Rehydrate the potatoes and onions. Fry in grease until done. Pour 2 well-blended eggs over it and continue frying until the eggs are done. Salt and pepper. Eat hot or cold.

POTATOES, ONIONS, AND BACON

    1   c crushed sliced or plain-dry diced potatoes
    1   T dried minced onion
    ¼   t garlic powder
    salt and pepper
    1 or 2 oz salt cured bacon, sliced thin

Rehydrate the potatoes and onions (with the garlic) in the water. Fry the bacon and then fry the rehydrated ingredients with them. If you are using TVP bacon (see page 35), add it at the last minute—after frying the potatoes and onions.

SWEET POTATOES AND FRUIT

    1   c diced cooked and dried sweet potatoes
    ¼   c raisins and dried apricots
    1   T brown sugar

Add 1¼ cups of water. A hot chicken or turkey gravy is good poured over this.

BEANS (also see pages 43 to 45)

BEEF AND BEANS NO. 1

    1   c dried and ground refried beans
    ¼   c dried, cooked, and slightly ground beef
    1   T dried minced onions
    salt and pepper

Add 1½ cups of water. You may need a bit more after or during cooking.

BEEF AND BEANS NO. 2

    1   c dried beans saturated in beef bouillon
    1   T dried, minced onions
    ¼   c dried cooked, and slightly ground beef
    salt and pepper

Add 1½ cups of water.

BEEF AND BEANS NO. 3

½ c dried beans saturated in beef bouillon
½ c dried beans saturated in brown sugar
¼ c dried, cooked, and slightly ground beef
salt and pepper

Add 1½ cups water.

REFRIED BEANS (page 43)

BEAN SALADS (page 44)

BEAN BALLS (page 44)

CHILI AND BEANS NO. 1
(see pages 21–22 and 40)

1 c cooked and dried kidney or pinto beans
1 package onion soup mix
1 beef bouillon cube or packet of dried
    beef bouillon
1 T dried bell pepper
1 t chili mix with tomatoes
    (or ¼ t chili powder)
2 T cornstarch
¼ t garlic chips or powder
½ t oregano

Add 2¼ cups of water.

CHILI AND BEANS NO. 2

1 c dried beans saturated in beef bouillon
1 T onions
1 package instant tomato soup
¼ c cooked and dried beef
½ t oregano
¼ t chili powder (or to taste)
salt and pepper

Add 2½ cups of water.

CHILI AND BEANS NO. 3

> 1   c dried beans saturated in a mixture of
>   beef bouillon and taco sauce or with
>   chili powder added to the bouillon
> ¼   c cooked and dried beef
> ½   t oregano
>   salt and pepper

Add 2½ cups of water.

CHILI AND BEANS NO. 4

Canned chili and beans are easily dried at home and easily carried (See page 21.)

BEAN SOUPS (pages 43 and 97)

BAKED BEANS (page 45)

A can of baked beans can be dried (see page 21) after first removing and clearing the fat from the can. If this is done, add 1 teaspoon of cornstarch to the dried mix when packaging. Weigh the beans first and afterwards; this is the weight of the water, less 10 percent, you should use to rehydrate. Here are some alternatives:

BAKED BEANS NO. 1

> 1   c cooked and dried small white beans
>   (or others)
> 2   T brown sugar
> 1   t cornstarch
> ¼   t sage
>   pinch of dried mustard

Add 2 cups of water.

BAKED BEANS NO. 2

> 1   c small white beans (or others)
>   saturated in brown sugar
> ¼   t sage
>   pinch of dried mustard
> 1   t cornstarch

Add 2 cups of water. Since the above is very sweet, half-saturated and half-plain cooked beans may be more to your liking. Salt-cured bacon can be added to these dishes to improve them. Or add a tablespoon of any grease.

RICE (see pages 52 to 55)

SPANISH RICE

Make this at home and dry it.

1   c rice
½   c tomato sauce
2   T dried minced onion
2   T dried crushed bell peppers
1   T paprika or chili powder to taste
½   t oregano
1   pinch garlic powder
salt

Add 1½ cups of water, bring to a simmer, and cook as basic rice. When done, dry it.

To cook on the trail, add 1¾ cups water. Give One Minute Boil (OMB), or cook until done.

CURRIED RICE

Add ½ teaspoon of curry powder to the above recipe and don't use the paprika or chili powder. Dried vegetables can be packaged with the dried curried rice.

CHICKEN AND PEAS RICE

Package together:

1   c cooked and dried basic rice
      (or use minute rice)
¼   c cooked and dried peas
½   oz cooked and dried chicken
1   t minced dried onion
2   chicken bouillon cubes or packets
      of dried chicken bouillon
salt and pepper

To cook, add 2 cups of water, OMB, and let sit 15 minutes. Or cook until done.

JAMBALAYA (SHRIMP)

Package together:

1 c cooked and dried basic rice
½ oz dried and ground shrimp
2 T dried tomato juice or 4 T dried tomato soup
1 T dried celery
1 t minced dried onions
1 t dried bell peppers
2 packets chicken broth
1 pinch of thyme

To cook: Add 1¾ cups of water, OMB, and sit for 15 to 20 minutes. NOTE: Jambalaya may be made with any meat or only with vegetables.

RICE WITH FRUIT AND NUTS

1 c cooked and dried basic rice
¼ c chopped nuts
¼ c raisins
¼ c fine chopped-dried peaches or apricots
1 t dried minced onions
¼ t curry powder
salt and pepper

To cook, add 1¾ cups of water. OMB and let sit 15 to 20 minutes.

CONGEE (see page 54)

CHICKEN CONGEE

Add to the basic recipe on page 54:

111

3 chicken bouillon cubes or packets
    of dried chicken broth
1 oz cooked and dried chicken,
    slightly ground
1 T minced dried onions
1 t parsley
pinch garlic powder
salt

Cook as basic congee.

SWEET CHICKEN CONGEE

Add 3 tablespoons of brown sugar to chicken congee.

TOFU CONGEE (BEAN CAKE CONGEE)
(2¾ oz)

Add 1 square freeze-dried Tofu (Koya Dofu) (see page 39) to the basic congee and 3 packets of chicken broth.

You may add Tofu to any of the following congees:

FISH CONGEE (1¾ oz)

Add to the basic congee:

¼ c dried bonita flakes
1   T minced dried onions
1   t parsley
salt

Cook as the basic congee.

SHRIMP CONGEE (2½ oz)

Add to the basic congee:

1 oz ground dry shrimp
1 t parsley
1 packet of dried shrimp broth
    or 2 packets of chicken broth

Cook as the basic congee.

SWEET CONGEE (LEMON)

Add to the basic congee:

> 3 T brown sugar
> 1 T lemon powder or crystals
> or ½ t unsweetened lemonade

Cook as the basic congee. Sweet congee can be varied with fruits or flavors.

BEEF CONGEE

Add to the basic congee:

> 3 packets beef broth or 1 oz cooked,
> dried, and ground beef
> 1 T dried minced onions
> 1 t dried parsley
> 1 oz cooked and dried beef

Cook as basic congee.

VEGETABLE CONGEE

Add the following to the basic congee:

> 2 to 3 oz dried vegetables, slightly ground
> 3 packets beef or chicken broth
> 1 T minced dried onions
> ½ t oregano

Cook as basic congee.

PASTA SAUCES AND GRAVIES
(for pasta, see pages 64 to 71)

Almost any pasta sauce or gravy can be made at home and dried as a leather. Various cheeses can and are used with pasta. The following suggestions are for 6 ounces of dry pasta, cooked in 1¾ to 2 cups of water.

They are usually best when the pasta is a thin spaghetti

or a narrow noodle. Where butter is called for (see page 87), bacon grease can be used if you cut the amounts in half.

PASTA CON BURRA E PEPE

Cook the pasta and add 2 tablespoons of melted "butter" and ½ teaspoon of ground pepper.

CON PARMIGIANO E BURRO

Cook the pasta and add 2 tablespoons of melted "butter." Then mix well with the pasta. Sprinkle grated cheese on top.

PASTA WITH GARLIC AND BUTTER

Before cooking the pasta, add ½ teaspoon of garlic powder to the water. Just before serving, pour 2 or 3 tablespoons of melted "butter" over the pasta.

PASTA MAITRE D'

Cook the pasta and while the pasta is sitting after the One Minute Boil (OMB), mix 1 teaspoon of dried lemon powder with 1 tablespoon of water and blend them well. Add 2 or 3 tablespoons of "butter" and 1 teaspoon of dried parsley and heat. Pour over the pasta before serving.

PASTA WITH OREGANO AND ONION

Add 1 tablespoon of dried minced onions and ½ teaspoon of ground oregano to the water before heating. Before serving the pasta, pour 2 tablespoons of melted "butter" over it and a bit of cheese.

PASTA AND MUSHROOMS

Instead of 2 cups, use 2¼ cups of water. Add 7 or 8 mushrooms (dried at home) to the water before heating. Pour 2 tablespoons of melted "butter" over the pasta and mushrooms before serving.

PASTA AND GROUND NUTS

Add 2 or 3 tablespoons of melted "butter" to the pasta and sprinkle with ground nuts.

PASTA WITH SOUR CREAM AND CHIVES

Mix a package of dry sour cream sauce with ½ cup water. Add a teaspoon of dried chives (if none in the sauce). Mix well together and let sit while the pasta is cooking. Just before serving, pour the cool or cold sour cream and chive mix over the pasta as you would any sauce or gravy. Dried minced onions can be substituted for the chives.

CHICKEN OR BEEF FLAVORED PASTA

Add 2 chicken or beef bouillon cubes or packs of dried bouillon to the water before heating. Pour 2 or 3 tablespoons of melted "butter" over the pasta before serving.

MACARONI AND CHEESE

Use any short macaroni. (Salad macaroni is good.) Begin with 6 ounces of macaroni and 2 cups of water. Use a packaged cheese sauce. Mix the sauce and let it sit while the pasta is cooking. When the pasta is done, stir the sauce into it. Sprinkle a bit of strong dried blue cheese if you want "a bite" to the dish. Onions mixed in the water before heating are good with this.

TOMATO-BASED SAUCES AND GRAVIES

Normally a commercial grocery sauce is used. For tomato, use a good instant tomato soup (see page 78). An excellent and light tomato sauce is:

LIGHT TOMATO SAUCE

¼ c good instant tomato soup
¼ c dry sour cream dressing
    (with chives or onions)
¼ c dried green olives (see page 40)

Mix the tomato soup with ¼ cup of hot water. When creamed, add ¾ cup of cool water. Add the sour cream dressing. Blend well together. Put the olives into the pasta water before heating. Then cook the pasta. Pour the sauce over the pasta before eating.

COMMERCIALLY DRIED SAUCES AND GRAVIES

Any dried sauce or gravy can be used on pasta (see page 70).

PASTA SOUPS (see page 71)

HASH

Hash usually means a dish made of chopped meats, normally leftovers, mixed with chopped vegetables and then fried. Gravy is occasionally used on hash. If several different vegetables are used and the gravy thinned a bit, the hash becomes similar to a stew.

Hash can be made with almost any vegetable. The following recipes call for potatoes or hominy, but any vegetable can be used. Dried squash, for example, is inexpensive and makes an unusual but decent hash.

CORNED-BEEF HASH

> 1 c dried diced cooked potatoes
> 2 oz dried and ground corned-beef jerky
> (cooked or "raw")
> 1 t dried minced onions
> salt and pepper

Rehydrate in 2 cups of water, about 2 hours at sea level, or OMB and let sit 15 minutes, or cook until ready. When rehydrated, drain and fry in grease.

ROAST-BEEF HASH

Use 2 ounces of cooked and dried, ground roast beef instead of the corned beef.

HOMINY AND BACON HASH

        1 c dried hominy
        2 oz salt-cured bacon, sliced thin
        salt and pepper

Rehydrate the hominy in 2 cups of water and treat as in the corned-beef hash recipe above. Remove the hominy from the pot, gently fry the bacon for a few minutes. Then add the hominy and fry it with the bacon.

STEWS (also see page 81)

The best light-pack stews are those made at home, for eating at home, with planned leftovers dried. It's worth remembering that stews made in this manner can also be used again at home.

However, the following recipes are for stews that are *assembled* from dried ingredients, then labeled and packaged at home for trail use. They are good and will serve well.

BASIC STEW

        ½ c dried vegetables
        ½ c diced dried potatoes
        2 oz dried cooked beef in small pieces
            or other meat option
        1 T dried minced onion
        2 beef bouillon cubes or packets of
            dried beef bouillon
        2 t cornstarch
        1 t dried parsley
        ½ t dried ground oregano (optional)
        ½ t thyme
        ¼ t garlic powder
        salt and pepper

To cook, mix with 2 cups of water.
The above can be varied in any way. If you like only

117

peas and carrots, use only peas and carrots. Instead of the seasonings called for, use grocery beef stew seasoning or any other that appeals to you. The meat can be any meat option. If using chicken or turkey instead of beef, substitute chicken bouillon for the beef bouillon.

IRISH (LAMB) STEW (also see page 100)

This is a dish that grew out of poverty, as many excellent ones did. Basically Irish stew is a soup or stew, depending on how much food is available and how many are to be fed. When drying lamb, you must be careful to use only very lean meat and get all the visible fat off. Lamb fat is very heavy tasting, and turns rancid quickly.

BASIC IRISH STEW

¾ c dried diced potatoes
2   oz dried, ground, and cooked
        lamb or mutton
2   T dried minced onions
1   t dried parsley
2   t cornstarch
pinch garlic powder
salt

To cook, mix with 2 cups of water.

IRISH STEW NO. 2

To the above add:

¼ c dried celery
1   chicken or beef bouillon cube
        or packet of dried broth

To cook, add 2 cups of water.

IRISH STEW NO. 3

To Irish Stew No. 2 add:

¼ c cooked and dried peas
Enough ground instant mashed potatoes
to fill the spaces between the other
ingredients in the mix

To cook, add 3 cups of water.

GREEK-STYLE LAMB STEW

To the basic Irish Stew recipe add:

¼ c cooked and dried peas
4 T tomato soup mix
1 chicken bouillon cube or packet
of dried bouillon

To cook, add 2 cups of water.

INDIAN STYLE LAMB STEW (CURRY)

To any recipe above add:

¼ c dried apples
¼ c raisins
¼ t curry powder (more if desired)

To cook, add 2 cups of water.

CHICKEN STEWS

Chicken stews may be assembled using any of the recipes above and substituting chicken or chicken flavored Textured Vegetable Protein (TVP) for the meat and chicken bouillon for the beef (see page 38). A quarter teaspoon of ginger is also good in a chicken stew.

CHICKEN AND PINEAPPLE STEW

1 c cooked and dried rice
2 oz heat-dried pineapple, well ground
2 oz dried cooked and ground chicken
   or TVP
2 chicken bouillon cubes or packets
   dried bouillon
1 T brown sugar
1 t minced dried onions
1 t cornstarch
1 pinch garlic
salt

To cook, add 2 cups of water.

TURKEY STEWS

These may be made as chicken stews above. Commercial dried turkey gravy should be used to replace the bouillon.

TURKEY OR CHICKEN, DRESSING AND GRAVY

½ c cooked, dried, and ground turkey or
   chicken, or 1 oz freeze-dried
¾ c bread stuffing, fairly tightly packed
1   package turkey or chicken gravy

To cook: bring ½ cup of water to a boil and mix the stuffing well with it. Set it aside. Make the gravy, putting the meat into the water before applying heat. Pour the meat and gravy over the stuffing, and apply a little heat afterwards, if necessary.

LENTIL STEW

Completely cook the lentils, using the recipe on the package, and dry them.

1   c cooked and dried lentils
2   oz dried, hard sausage, sliced very thin
1   T dried minced onion
2   t cornstarch
½   t oregano or thyme
    salt and pepper

To cook, add 2 cups of water. For slightly better results, boil the hard sausage for a few minutes first.

SWEET DESSERTS

A number of ingredients or packaged goods, and a number of different methods can be used to make light-pack desserts that are easy to make and good to eat.

The basis of many can be one of the various instant puddings or pie fillings available at the grocery or delicatessen.

These can be made without heat and allowed to sit and jell. If the package instructions call for milk, use instant dry nonfat milk, because some will not jell without the calcium of the milk.

A crushed graham cracker, sugar cookie, oatmeal cookie, etc. (see page 144) "crust" can be made by mixing the crushed cookies with some vegetable shortening and spreading the mix around the sides of the pan.

This takes a bit of work and is unnecessary, unless having a "crust" on the bottom of the dessert is important to you. Sprinkle the crushed cookies on top of the dessert instead, or mix them into the dessert just before serving.

The puddings can have rum, mint, anise (licorice taste), or other flavoring added to them. Use extracts from the spice section of the grocery. Mint is often easy to find on the trail. Mint tea can be made and when cooled the tea used to make the pudding.

Here's a recipe for a very sweet cream that can be carried:

1 oz confectioners' or powdered sugar
2 oz ground instant nonfat milk

Grind the two together to get a good mix. When it's ready to use, add 2 or 3 ounces of water and stir well.

"Sweet" sour cream is often available in dry form. Be certain the dry sour cream is sweet and doesn't have onions or other surprises added to it. Onions will ruin the dessert.

Dried nondairy whipped "cream" is available. Use instant nonfat dried milk where milk is called for, and only use ½ or ¾ the water called for. Whip it a bit with a fork to speed the jelling. This doesn't result in a whipped "cream" when done this way, but it's a good, sweet, thick mixture.

Dried fruits (see page 46) can be the basis of excellent and easy-to-prepare desserts. They can be rehydrated and the extra water used to make one of the "sweet creams" above.

Crushed cookies can be added just before eating. A crushed cookie, brown sugar, and milk mush is also good.

Blueberries and cream? Strawberries and cream? With crushed cookies? Call them "tarts."

Compotes are dried apples or other dried fruits mixed with sugar and water, boiled and then allowed to cool. They are good. Cinnamon is a good spice for most of these, ginger often a pleasant change. Nutmeg or allspice are good, too.

Thick fruit soups are good, and the thicker they are the more they become a compote.

A grape nut "mush" is made with grape nuts and a fruit juice and allowed to stand until a mush. This is good, especially if sweet cream is poured over it.

Condensed mince meat is available commercially. Mix it with water and bring it to a boil. Add fruits and nuts if you like.

How about hot chocolate with a bit of coffee and rum in it?

Any of these can be made quickly and with very little fuss. They should be packaged at home. When the ingredients should be kept apart during preparation, put them in an extra bag, instead of the package bag.

Well-aged fruit cakes run from 105 to 120 calories per ounce. A nondairy whip (190 calories per dry ounce) over them is excellent.

BETTIES

Betties can be packaged at home in a number of flavors.

BROWN BETTY

1   c dried bread in small pieces
½   c dried bread crumbs
½   c heat-dried apples in small pieces
¼   c raisins
⅓   c brown sugar
1   t cinnamon
salt

To cook, add 2 cups of water. Give One Minute Boil (OMB) and let sit 15 minutes. Or cook until done.

PINEAPPLE BETTY

1   c dried bread in small pieces
½   c dried bread crumbs
½   c heat-dried pineapple slightly ground
½   c heat-dried apples slightly ground
⅓   c white or brown sugar
1   t cinnamon
salt

Cook as above.

PART
IV
NUTRITION

GENERAL NUTRITION INFORMATION

WATER AND SALT

If at all possible, "Drink when you are thirsty!"

To function properly, the human body needs from 2 to 3 quarts of water per day, when *at rest*. About half of this, 1 quart or so, normally comes from food. You have to drink the rest, whether it's soda, tea, lemonade, or plain, cool water.

The first or second day constipation that affects many people on outdoor trips is often caused by lack of water. The bowels need from ½ cup to, perhaps, a cup of water to function normally. In addition, water must be taken in for other, priority, needs such as sweat. (Diarrhea is quite another matter. A good bit of water is necessary to replace the water lost in this manner. Adjust your intake to the amount lost and drink it reasonably soon, but in small amounts at a time. Include a little salt with the water intake.)

Whatever your water intake habits at home, on the trail requirements are usually considerably higher.

Lack of water causes, first, thirst. Then if the water is not taken, the lack of water causes fatigue, and later dizziness, and still later delirium and coma, followed in extreme instances by death.

In extreme circumstances, water lost through sweat can reach a quart or more in an hour. Heavy sweating also causes loss of salt. The salt should be replaced because a lack of salt can also cause fatigue, dizziness, and exhaustion.

The amount of salt to take is an individual matter and will take some experimenting on your part.

If you have been sweating and you're tired, cramps can be caused by drinking large (2 or 3 cups) quantities of unsalted water at one time.

If it's very dry weather, whether hot or cold, higher than normal water loss occurs as the dry air "leeches" water from your skin, without noticeable perspiration. Another point is that heavy work causes you to breathe through your mouth, which also increases your water loss.

A good rule is to drink ½ cup or a cup of water at a time, whenever you're thirsty. If you've been sweating a lot, replace the salt lost. Take a bit (½ teaspoon or a salt tablet for this purpose) with the water.

Water has to get to the stomach to do any good. Swirling some around in the mouth isn't going to help, however good it makes the mouth feel.

Whatever your water or salt habits at home, when outdoors on a hot day, take some salt, and drink when you're thirsty.

DRINKABLE WATER

Water to drink (or cook with) should be "pure," free from bacterial contamination. If in doubt about any water, purify it with halazone or iodine tablets (available at any drug store). Or boil the water for ten minutes, which takes fuel.

The tablets give the water a unique taste; lemonade, tea, or other flavoring can be added to mask the taste. An easier way to get accustomed to halazoned or iodined water is to sip it occasionally a day or two before the trip. The taste will "disappear" in the sense that you won't notice it as much.

WHEN TO EAT

Normal mealtimes established by tradition are breakfast, lunch, and dinner. This is a good general routine to follow whether at home or on the trail. If a fourth meal is added, try to space all four meals equal distance apart.

The higher the food intake at any one time, the more blood is needed in the stomach area for digestion. Whatever other activity you are engaged in, the heart will pump this additional blood supply to the stomach area.

If you eat heartily and immediately engage in a heavy activity, your heart is going to work considerably harder, and you are more likely to get tired, or make an error.

A more or less usable guideline might be: Half an hour of light activity after a light meal, an hour after a medium one, and an hour and a half after a reasonably heavy meal.

Many people have taken to having the long, contemplative break at midday and sleeping shortly after dinner. It seems an excellent idea.

Continuous heavy snacking—to increase your energy —without suitable rest periods is inadvisable. It can do the opposite—slow you down. (In very strenuous activities—such as mountaineering—the lack of energy may be due to a lack of water and salt.)

If you are going to continuously snack, it is likely best to restrict yourself to very small amounts of sugars and hard candies at any one time.

To increase or maintain your energy, remember that carbohydrates are quicker to digest than protein or fat (see upcoming sections). Of the carbohydrates, dextrose is the fastest, however it takes from an hour or two, or even more, for the dextrose to be available for "energy."

Proteins take several hours or more, and fat doesn't normally *begin* to digest for an hour and a half.

WHAT TO EAT

It's nutritionally sound to carry dried-food weights as follows:

> 2 or more ounces of dried meats or eggs (peas, beans, or nuts can be substituted)
> 4 or more ounces of dried vegetables or fruits
> 3 or more ounces of dried milk or hard cheese
> 4 or more ounces of any of the various grain products
> Plus other foods, including fats and beverages as needed to provide energy and food values, for each day on the trail.

When these are rehydrated and cooked, the list corresponds to the same one home economists recommend for normal daily activities:

> 2 or more servings of food from the meat group
> 4 or more servings from the vegetable and fruit group
> Food from the milk group
> 4 or more servings of food from the bread and cereal group plus other foods, etc.

PROTEIN

To figure how much protein is needed per day, adults should multiply body weight by .47 grams. Growing youngsters need .7 grams per pound of body weight. For example, a growing person who weighs 130 pounds would need (130 × .7 = 91) 91 grams of protein, which equals 3.2 ounces (91 × 28.35; there are 28.35 grams per ounce).

Protein is necessary to the body's function and growth. The body does not store protein. If there is no immediate need, the protein is turned into "sugar" and used for energy. If not needed for energy, it is turned into fat and stored against future energy needs. It cannot be converted back into protein.

Twenty years ago, it was thought that increased physical effort required increased protein intake. Today, that theory is considered invalid, with the following two exceptions: (1) increased activity that builds muscles, and (2) increased activity that causes heavy sweating. Protein is needed to build the muscles, and a protein derivative (nitrogen) is lost in sweat.

If you are sweating heavily, you might add an ounce or two of protein per day. The protein necessary to build muscles is allowed for in the ration for growing persons (.7 grams per day), noted above. But if you are an adult, you can also build muscles. So muscle-building activity calls for an increase in protein.

Please note that there is no panic about the intake of protein. The body can do without it for a few days. Some authorities once thought as long as a couple of weeks. But fatigue will set in quickly if the protein deficiency is extended over a couple of days.

FATS

The body needs the values that fats provide, and fat is the lightest food in terms of calories per ounce. It takes the body over an hour and a half to begin to digest fat. But 1 gram of fat has 9 calories, and an ounce has 250.

The body transforms the fat into a form of sugar and then if this isn't needed, it becomes fat, which is stored on the body.

If you are working in cold, your body needs some fat intake. And if you are outdoors on a series of cold and wintery days, fat should be an increased part of your diet.

The body needs carbohydrates in fairly large proportion to fully digest fats. If enough carbohydrates are not taken, fat alone can cause acid indigestion, and simply pass through without contributing to your body's functions.

CARBOHYDRATES

Carbohydrates are defined as foods containing starch and sugar. Carbohydrates in the form of dextrose are the easiest and fastest to digest.

The major portion (traditionally ⅔) of the diet is composed of carbohydrates such as grains, potatoes, and fruits. Here's a good rule of thumb:

⅙ protein foods
⅙ fats (fat is also part of many foods in addition to oils, etc.)
⅔ carbohydrates, of which ¼ to ⅕ are sugar(s), and the balance starches.

HOW MUCH TO CARRY

The actual amount to carry has to be worked out in testing by each individual. The goal is to return from a trip with exactly zero food, except for emergency rations. Every extra ounce or pound is a waste of pack space and the energy used to carry it.

An easy way to start is to figure how much you eat at home, by weight, and then pack 20 to 25 percent of that weight in dried foods. You might be a bit hungry the last day of the trip, but you'll also be a bit lighter on the scales.

If you carry a little extra fat around your middle, it's good for around 248 calories per ounce. I base this estimate on beef fat (suet) as I don't know of, nor do I think I want to know of, any tests with human fat. If you are only 1 pound overweight, that could be worth about 4,000 calories.

If the above method doesn't appeal to you, here's one I've adapted from *Energy, Work, and Leisure* by Durnin, J.V.G. and R. Passmore (Heinemann Educations Books). It requires a minute of math: If you know your body weight, use the chart below. (Note: If you weigh 180 pounds and are 20 pounds overweight, figure 160.)

Males, adult:	body weight	times	16 to 21	calories	per	day
Males, growing:	" "	"	25 to 29	"	"	"
Females, adult:	" "	"	14 to 18	"	"	"
Females, growing:	" "	"	20 to 24	"	"	"

You can add 50 to 60 percent to the maximum figure for a very strenuous day. If possible, eat half the extra the night before and half the evening of the strenuous day.

It's my own opinion that most people doing normal outdoor activities are comfortable closer to the middle range (or slightly below) of calories per pound per day, in the table above. **If the math bugs you, just carry about 2 pounds of dried food per day for a 2- or 3-day trip. Weigh what you come home with, and make adjustments for the next trip.**

One final word. I've made a serious effort to keep this discussion understandable and usable. Some people enjoy counting calories and proteins. If you want to learn more on the subject, many good books are available. Nutritionists and home economists in your area may also be of help.

In practice, try to keep the weight and bulk of the pack down. Eat about the way you do at home. Drink when you are thirsty, and sleep when you are tired.

MENU PLANNING

For a short, 2- or 3-day trip, very little thought is required. List the kinds of meals you want. Then list what you have in your larder and what you plan to make or buy.

Break the meals down by the days, trying for some variety and nutritional balance. Then package the food and label it. It's helpful to carry a small card that lists your planned menu by the day and by the meal. Then after eating you may want to make notes on proportions for future use, and may want to note how well you liked the meal.

For longer trips the same procedure is useful, and to simplify menu planning, it is a good idea to work in groups of days, say a 4-day menu and then simply repeat it or portions of it on a 5- to 8-day trip, twice on a 12-day trip, and so forth.

Avoid a 7-day menu on long trips. With one, you are eating the same meal every Sunday.

One other thought—foods that are repeated often wear better on the palate if they are bland. A few spices can be carried for variations.

FOOD VALUES PER DRIED OUNCE
(also see pages 56 to 58)

The quickest way to figure food values of trail foods is to consider that all dried foods average 115 to 120 calories per dried ounce. To use this figure as a basis, carry $\frac{1}{6}$ fat, $\frac{1}{6}$ protein, and $\frac{2}{3}$ carbohydrates. The averages will, if your menu is reasonably varied, work themselves out to about those figures.

TABLES OF FOOD VALUES

Following are listings for most, perhaps all, of the basic foods that you might want to carry. Also, farther on, is a listing of the food values of a number of grocery items and 102 commercially packaged trail foods.

These lists show values for dried foods by the *dry ounce*, as carried. The listing offers a means of making comparisons and helps in making knowledgeable choices, and may also act as a shopping list or at least an idea list.

Also refer to the "Table of Contents" as well as the "Index" in this book for other explanations.

The following figures on basic and miscellaneous foods have either been adapted by me from the Composition of Foods, Agriculture Handbook No. 8, U.S. Department of Agriculture, or from information supplied by the manufacturers. Most of the figures given for the values of commercial trail foods were compiled by Dr. William W. Fogerty, M.D., President of Indiana Camp Supply, Inc.

For ease of comparison, all food values are per dry ounce (unless otherwise noted).

I. FOOD VALUES OF MILK, MILK PRODUCTS, & EGGS

Per Dry Ounce (except as noted)	Total Calories	Grams Protein	Grams Fat	Grams Carbo-hydrates
Buttermilk	110	9.7	1.5	14.2
Chocolate, milk*				
Cheeses (as sold):				
Blue, Roquefort type	104	6.1	8.6	—
Brick	104	6.3	8.6	—
Cheddar (American)	113	7.1	9.1	—
Cottage cheese	117	15.0	4.6	3.2
Parmesan (grated)	111	10.1	7.3	.8
Swiss (US)	105	7.8	7.9	—
Pasteurized process cheese:				
American	105	6.6	8.5	—
Pimiento (American)	105	6.5	8.6	—
Swiss (US)	101	7.5	7.6	2.0
Pasteurized process cheese food:				
American	92	5.6	6.8	—
Spread	82	4.5	6.1	—
Cocoa & chocolate drinks:				
With nonfat milk	102	5.3	.8	20.1
Without milk	98	1.1	.6	25.3
Mix for hot chocolate	111	2.7	3.0	20.9
Cocoa, dry powder:				
High fat, plain	85	5.0	6.7	13.7
Processed with alkali	84	5.0	6.7	12.8
Medium fat	75	4.9	5.4	14.6
Low fat	62	5.4	3.6	15.3
Cream, nondairy:				
Common	144	2.4	7.6	17.4
Containing sodium hexameta-phosphate	144	3.9	7.8	15.1
Eggs:				
Whole	168	13.3	11.7	1.2
Whole, stabilized—glucose reduced	173	13.9	12.1	.7
White, flakes	99	21.3	—	1.5
White, powder	105	22.7	—	1.6
Yolk	188	9.4	16.1	.7
Milk:				
Dry, whole	142	7.5	7.8	10.8

I. FOOD VALUES OF MILK, MILK PRODUCTS, & EGGS
(*Continued*)

Per Dry Ounce	Total Calories	Grams Protein	Grams Fat	Grams Carbohydrates
Nonfat	102	10.2	.2	14.6
Malted milk	116	4.1	2.4	20.1

* *See "Sugars & Sweets" table on upcoming pages.*

II. FOOD VALUES OF MEATS

Per Dry Ounce	Total Calories	Grams Protein	Grams Fat	Grams Carbohydrates
Bacon, fatty	220	2.8	23.1	.2
Lean (50% meat)	175	11.4	13.7	—
Beef	122	19.6	4.3	—
Meatballs	119	13.6	3.1	6.8
Chicken	120	20.6	3.4	—
Deer*	117	20.1	3.5	—
Fish, all types lean fish (under 1% when fresh), including shell fish	100	21.1	.9	—
Lamb	125	19.6	4.6	—
Pemmican†	185	10.0	15.0	—
Turkey	126	20.9	4.0	—
Textured Vegetable Protein (TVP)‡	105	21.2	—	4.3

Note: The above figures are averages, based on efficient drying, using the leanest meat possible, and removing all visible fat. If figures are used to evaluate commercially dried meats, there should be no additives. Adding various fillers can cut the above values by as much as 40 percent.

* *Most game will run close to these figures.*

† *Based on 42% dried beef and 58% fat. If the dried beef ratio is increased, the total calorie count comes down and the protein count goes up. Commercial meat bars have around 160 calories, 13 to 15 grams of protein, and 11 to 14 grams of fat. If the commercial meat bar has other ingredients, the entire food value count is reduced.*

‡ *Assuming the TVP is based on soy proteinate. If it is based on other soy products, the food values are slightly reduced.*

III. FOOD VALUES OF VEGETABLES

Per Dry Ounce	Total Calories	Grams Protein	Grams Fat	Grams Carbo-hydrates
Asparagus	59	5.8	.5	11.8
Bamboo shoots	55	5.2	.6	11.6
Beans, common:				
White	96	6.3	.5	17.4
Red	97	6.4	.4	17.6
Pinto/calico/red Mexican	99	6.5	.3	18.1
Others	96	6.3	.4	17.4
Beans, lima	98	5.8	.5	18.1
Beans, lima/flour	97	6.0	.4	17.8
Beans, mung	96	6.9	.4	17.1
Beans, soy (beans)	114	9.7	5.0	9.5
Tofu (curds)	106	11.5	6.2	3.5
Flours:				
Full fat	119	10.4	5.6	8.6
Hi High fat	108	11.7	3.4	9.4
Low fat	101	12.3	1.9	10.4
Defatted	92	13.3	.3	10.8
Beets	73	2.7	—	16.8
Blackeyed peas (see cowpeas)				
Broadbeans	96	7.1	.5	16.5
Broccoli/trimmed	61	6.8	.6	3.9
Brussel sprouts	68	7.4	.6	6.6
Cabbage	59	3.0	—	20.0
Carrots	75	2.0	—	9.5
Cauliflower, trimmed	54	5.4	.4	11.5
Celeriac	73	3.3	.6	7.7
Celery	49	2.6	—	11.2
Chard, Swiss	55	5.3	.7	10.0
Chayote	65	1.4	—	16.5
Cherimoya	87	1.2	.4	22.3
Chervil	69	4.1	1.1	9.3
Chickpeas (garbanzos)	102	5.8	1.4	17.3
Chicory greens	56	4.6	.7	9.5
Chives	63	4.0	.7	12.8
Cottonseed flour	101	13.6	1.9	9.2

Per Dry Ounce	Total Calories	Grams Protein	Grams Fat	Grams Carbo-hydrates
Cowpeas, including black-eyed peas	97	6.4	.4	17.5
Dandelion greens	69	4.1	1.1	14.3
Endive	52	4.4	.3	10.7
Fennel	57	5.7	.8	10.3
Garbanzos (see chickpeas)				
Garlic cloves	91	4.1	.1	20.5
Grits (see corn grits)				
Hominy grits (see corn grits)				
Kale	65	6.5	1.0	11.2
Leeks	79	3.4	.4	16.8
Lettuce, crisphead	43	3.0	.3	6.5
Looseleaf	51	3.7	.9	9.7
Lima beans (see beans, lima)				
Mushrooms	58	5.6	.6	9.2
Okra	69	4.0	.2	15.8
Onions	99	2.5	.4	23.2
Parsley	66	5.4	.9	12.8
Parsnips	89	2.0	.6	19.9
Peas	96	6.8	.4	17.1
Peppers, hot (chili)	91	3.7	2.6	16.9
Peppers, sweet green	59	3.2	.5	12.9
Pigeonpeas	97	5.8	.4	18.1
Popcorn	103	3.4	1.3	20.4
Potatoes	103	2.0	.2	23.8
Potato flour	100	2.3	.2	22.6
Pumpkin (no seeds)	60	2.3	.2	14.8
Radishes	46	2.3	.2	7.5
Sorghum, grain	94	3.1	1.0	20.7
Squash, summer (no seeds)	53	3.0	.3	11.9
Sweet potatoes	105	1.2	.2	22.3
Tapioca	100	.2	—	24.5
Taros	90	1.7	.2	21.6
Tomatoes	60	3.0	.5	12.7
Tomato juice (crystals)	86	3.3	.6	19.3
Turnips	68	2.2	—	15.0
Yams	94	2.0	.2	21.6

IV. FOOD VALUES OF FRUITS

Per Dry Ounce	Total Calories	Grams Protein	Grams Fat	Grams Carbo-hydrates
Apples (2.5%, heat-dried)	100	.4	.6	26.1
Apples (25%, sun-dried)	78	.3	.5	20.4
Apricots (3.5%, heat-dried)	94	1.6	.3	24.0
Apricots (25%, sun-dried)	74	1.4	.1	18.8
Avocados (all commercial)	158	2.0	15.5	5.8
California (Fuerte)	158	2.0	15.7	5.7
Florida	140	1.5	12.0	9.7
Bananas	85	1.0	.2	22.1
Blackberries (dewberries, youngberries)	84	1.8	1.3	18.9
Blueberries	85	.9	.7	20.1
Boysenberries	79	2.0	.5	18.9
Breadfruit	88	1.4	—	22.4
Cantaloupe (see muskmelon)				
Casaba melon (see muskmelon)				
Cherries, sour	81	1.7	.4	22.4
Sweet	84	1.6	.4	20.9
Candied	96	.1	—	24.6
Citron, candied	89	—	—	22.8
Coconut, meat:				
Unsweetened	188	2.0	18.4	6.5
Sweetened, shredded	155	1.0	11.1	15.1
Cranberries	104	.8	1.9	23.9
Currants, black	77	2.4	.1	18.7
Red, white	77	2.2	.3	18.7
Dates, no pits (22% water)	78	.6	.1	20.1
Elderberries	84	3.0	.6	19.2
Figs (23%, sun-dried)	78	1.2	.4	19.6
(4%, heat-dried)	86	1.3	.3	21.7
Grapefruit	68	.8	.2	17.7
Crystals	103	1.5	—	25.6
Guavas	84	1.1	.8	20.3
Honeydew melon (see muskmelon)				
Jujube (Chinese date)	72	.9	.3	18.6
Kumquats	81	1.1	.1	21.3
Lemons, whole	46	1.9	.5	14.0
Lemonade	99	—	—	
Loganberries	84	1.3	.8	20.0

Per Dry Ounce	Total Calories	Grams Protein	Grams Fat	Grams Carbo-hydrates
Loquats	78	.6	.3	20.1
Mangos	84	.9	.5	21.3
Muskmelons (cantaloupe & other netted varieties)	66	1.6	.2	16.6
Casaba	61	2.7	—	14.7
Honeydew	70	1.7	.7	16.3
Olives:				
Green, pickled, no pits	128	1.6	13.9	1.4
Black, pickled, no pits	168	1.1	18.4	2.9
Greek style, no pits (43%)	96	.6	10.1	2.5
(4%, heat-dried)	159	1.0	16.8	4.1
Orange, crystals	107	1.4	.5	25.2
Papaws	88	5.3	.9	17.3
Papayas	73	1.1	—	18.5
Peaches (25%, sun-dried)	74	.9	.5	19.3
(3%, heat-dried)	96	1.4	.3	24.9
Pears (26%, sun-dried)	76	.9	.2	19.1
(4%, heat-dried)	83	1.0	.6	20.9
Pineapple	79	.6	.3	20.8
Plums:				
Damson	82	.6	—	22.0
Japanese, hybrid	78	.8	.3	19.9
Prune-type	84	.9	.2	22.1
Prunes (28%, sofenized, no pits)	72	.6	.2	20.5
(2.5%, heat-dried, no pits)	98	.9	.1	25.8
Raisins (18%, sun-dried)	82	.7	—	21.9
Raspberries, black	89	1.8	1.7	19.2
Red	82	1.0	.7	19.5
Strawberries	66	1.2	.9	15.9
Youngberries (see blackberries)				

Food values are for foods efficiently dried, either as given (commercial) or, if home dried, with 4 percent moisture. If products are purchased freeze-dried they have about 3 percent higher food values (unless noted here *as* freeze-dried).

V. FOOD VALUES OF GRAIN
AND GRAIN PRODUCTS

Per Dry Ounce	Total Calories	Grams Protein	Grams Fat	Grams Carbo-hydrates
Alimentary paste (see pasta)				
Barley, pearled, light	99	2.3	.3	22.3
Pot, scotch	99	2.7	.3	21.9
Bran:				
Sugar, malt extract	68	3.6	.9	21.1
Sugar, defatted wheat germ	68	3.1	.9	22.3
Flakes, 40% bran	86	2.8	.5	22.8
Flakes, raisins	81	2.4	.4	22.5
Breads, cracked wheat (all dried)	108	3.6	.9	15.8
French, Vienna (sourdough)	107	3.5	1.2	21.4
Italian	108	3.6	.3	22.2
Raisin	108	2.7	1.2	22.1
Rye, American	100	3.7	.5	21.5
Rye, Pumpernickel	100	3.7	.5	21.4
Salt rising	116	3.4	1.0	21.9
White (3–4% nonfat milk)	110	3.6	1.3	20.9
Whole wheat (2% nonfat milk)	102	4.4	1.3	20.0
Whole wheat (water)	101	3.8	1.1	20.7
Bread crumbs	111	3.6	1.3	20.8
Bread stuffing mix	105	3.7	1.1	20.5
Breakfast cereals (see corn, rice, wheat, also bran and farina)				
Buckwheat, whole grain	95	3.3	.7	20.7
Flour, dark	94	3.3	.7	20.4
Flour, light	98	1.8	.3	22.5
Bulgar wheat:				
Hard winter, red	100	3.2	.4	21.4
White	101	2.9	.3	22.1
Cake mixes:				
Angel food	109	2.4	—	25.1
Chocolate malt	117	1.1	3.0	22.4
Coffee cake	122	1.7	3.1	21.9
Cupcake mix	124	1.0	3.9	21.4
Devil's food	115	1.4	3.3	21.8
Gingerbread	120	1.5	2.9	22.2
Honeyspice	126	1.2	4.0	21.6
Marble	120	1.4	3.8	21.4
White	123	1.2	3.4	22.2

Per Dry Ounce	Total Calories	Grams Protein	Grams Fat	Grams Carbo-hydrates
Yellow	124	1.1	3.6	22.0
Cake icings (see cake icing mixes, candy, sugars, & sweets table)				
Cereals, breakfast (see corn, oats, rice, wheat, also bran, farina)				
Cookies (see sugars and sweets table)				
Corn, sweet	84	3.1	.5	20.1
Corn flour	104	2.2	.7	21.7
Corn grits, degermed	103	2.5	.2	22.1
Cornmeal:				
Whole ground, unbolted	101	2.6	1.1	20.9
Bolted, nearly whole	103	2.6	1.0	21.1
Degermed	103	2.2	.3	22.2
Corn products:				
Used as breakfast cereals (for cornmeal, see vegetables table)				
Flakes	109	2.2	.1	24.2
Flakes, sugar-covered	109	1.2	—	25.9
Puffed	113	2.3	1.2	22.9
Shredded	110	2.0	.1	24.6
Cornstarch	103	.1	—	24.8
Crackers (as sold or made):				
Animal	122	1.9	2.7	22.6
Butter	130	2.0	5.0	19.1
Cheese	136	3.2	6.0	17.1
Graham, plain	109	2.7	2.7	20.8
Chocolate covered	135	1.4	6.6	19.3
Sugar, honey coated	117	1.9	3.2	21.6
Saltines	123	2.6	3.4	20.3
Sandwich, Peanut/cheese	139	4.3	6.8	15.9
Soda	124	2.6	3.7	20.0
Whole wheat	114	2.4	3.9	19.3
Farina, quick cooking & instant	103	3.2	.3	21.8
Macaroni (see pasta)				
Millet	93	2.8	.8	20.7
Noodles (see pasta)				

V. FOOD VALUES OF GRAIN
AND GRAIN PRODUCTS (Continued)

Per Dry Ounce	Total Calories	Grams Protein	Grams Fat	Grams Carbo-hydrates
Oats:				
Oat cereal, wheat germ, & soy grits	108	5.8	2.6	16.6
Flakes, instant	109	4.2	1.1	20.5
White wheat cereal	103	4.2	1.4	19.4
Oatmeal (rolled oats)	110	4.0	2.1	19.3
Pancake mix (plain)	101	2.4	15.0	21.4
Pasta (all types):				
With egg	109	3.6	1.2	21.4
Without egg	104	3.5	.5	21.3
Pastinas (see pasta)				
Popcorn (unpopped)	103	3.4	1.3	20.4
Pudding mixes (see candy, sweets, and sugars tables)				
Rice:				
Brown	102	2.1	.5	21.9
White, fully milled common (not instant)	103	1.9	.1	22.8
White, fully milled, instant	106	2.1	—	23.4
Mochi Gomi	102	1.6	.3	22.6
Rice bran	78	3.8	4.5	14.4
Rice products (used as hot breakfast foods)	109	1.7	—	24.4
Rice products used as ready-to-eat breakfast foods:				
Flakes	111	1.7	—	24.9
Puffed	113	1.7	.1	25.4
Shredded	111	1.5	—	25.2
Rusk	119	3.9	2.5	20.1
Rye, whole grain	95	3.4	.5	20.8
Flours, light	101	2.7	.3	22.1
Medium	99	3.2	.5	21.2
Dark	93	4.6	.7	19.3
Rye wafers (crisps)	98	3.7	.3	21.6
Spaghetti (see pasta)				
Wheat, whole grain:				
Hard, red, spring	94	4.0	.6	19.6

V. FOOD VALUES OF GRAIN
AND GRAIN PRODUCTS (Continued)

Per Dry Ounce	Total Calories	Grams Protein	Grams Fat	Grams Carbo-hydrates
Hard, red, winter	94	3.5	.5	20.3
Soft, red, winter	92	2.9	.6	20.4
White	95	2.7	.6	21.4
Duram	94	3.6	.7	19.9
Wheat flours:				
Whole (hard wheat)	104	3.4	.4	21.0
Soft wheat	103	2.8	.3	21.7
All-purpose	103	3.0	.3	21.6
Bread flour	104	3.3	.3	21.1
Gluten (45% gluten)	107	11.7	.5	13.4
Wheat germ	103	7.5	3.1	13.2
Wheat products used as hot breakfast cereals:				
Rolled wheat	96	2.8	.6	21.6
Whole meal	96	3.8	.6	20.5
Wheat used mainly as ready-to-eat breakfast cereals:				
Flakes	100	2.9	.5	22.8
Germ, toasted	111	8.5	3.3	14.1
Puffed	103	4.3	.4	22.2
Shredded	100	2.8	.6	22.6
and barley (malted) flakes	111	2.5	.4	23.9
Wildrice	111	4.0	.2	21.4

VI. FOOD VALUES OF FATS & OILS

Per Dry Ounce	Total Calories	Grams Protein	Grams Fat	Grams Carbo-hydrates
Bacon grease*	210	Unk.	23.3	—
Butter oil, clarified	248	—	28.0	—
Fats, vegetable, cooking	250	—	28.2	—
Lard	256	—	28.2	—
Margarine	204	.2	22.9	—
Oils, salad, cooking	250	—	28.2	—

* Bacon grease figures vary depending on "scrap" bacon included in the grease.

VII. FOOD VALUES OF CANDY, SUGAR, & SWEETS

Per Dry Ounce	Total Calories	Grams Protein	Grams Fat	Grams Carbo-hydrates
Cake icing mixes:				
Chocolate fudge	116	.7	.3	24.5
Creamed fudge	109	.9	2.1	24.1
Candy:				
Butterscotch	113	—	1.0	26.9
Candy corn (see chocolate-coated fondant)				
Carmel	113	1.1	2.9	21.7
Chocolate:				
Bittersweet	135	2.2	11.3	13.2
Semisweet	144	1.2	10.1	16.1
Sweet	150	1.2	9.9	16.4
Milk chocolate, plain	147	2.2	9.1	16.1
With almonds	151	2.6	10.1	14.5
With peanuts	154	4.0	10.8	12.6
Chocolate coated:				
Almonds	161	3.5	12.4	11.2
Fudge	122	1.1	4.5	20.7
Coconut center	124	.8	5.0	20.4
Fondant	116	.5	3.0	22.9
Peanuts	159	4.7	11.7	11.1
Raisins	121	1.5	4.9	19.9
Gumdrops	99	—	.2	24.8
Hard candy	109	—	.3	27.6
Jelly beans	104	—	.1	26.4
Mints, uncoated (see chocolate-coated fondant)				
Peanut bars	146	5.0	9.1	13.4
Peanut brittle	119	1.6	3.0	22.9
Sugar coated				
Almonds	129	2.2	5.3	19.9
Chocolate disks	132	1.5	5.6	19.9
Chewing gum (with sugar)	90	—	—	
Chocolate, milk (see candy)				
Cookies:				
Assorted	136	1.4	5.7	20.1
Brownies, with nuts	138	1.8	8.9	14.4
Butter, rich	130	1.7	4.8	20.1
Chocolate	130	1.7	4.5	20.3

VII. FOOD VALUES OF CANDY, SUGAR, & SWEETS

Per Dry Ounce	Total Calories	Grams Protein	Grams Fat	Grams Carbo-hydrates
Chocolate chip	146	1.5	8.5	17.0
Coconut bars	140	1.8	6.9	18.1
Fig bars	102	1.2	1.6	21.4
Gingersnaps	119	1.6	2.5	22.6
Macaroons	135	1.5	6.6	18.7
Marshmallow	116	1.1	3.8	20.5
Molasses	120	1.8	3.0	21.6
Oatmeal, with raisins	128	1.8	4.4	20.8
Peanut cookies	134	2.8	5.4	19.0
Raisin cookies	107	1.3	1.5	22.9
Sandwich	140	1.4	6.4	19.6
Shortbread	141	2.0	6.6	18.4
Sugar, soft	126	1.7	4.8	19.3
Sugar, hard	138	1.4	5.5	20.8
Vanilla wafers	131	1.5	4.6	21.1
Gelatin dessert powder	105	2.7	—	24.9
Ginger, candied	96	—	—	24.7
Honey	86	—	—	—
Jams & preserves	77	.2	—	19.8
Molasses, cane:				
Light	71	—	—	18.4
Medium	66	—	—	17.0
Blackstrap	60	—	—	15.6
Barbados	77	—	—	19.9
Pudding mixes:				
Starch base:				
Chocolate, instant	101	.9	.5	25.9
Veg. gum base:				
Custard	109	—	—	28.1
Rennin products:				
Dessert mixes:				
Chocolate	110	.8	.9	25.9
Other flavors	109	—	—	28.1
Syrups:				
Cane	74	—	—	19.2
Maple	71	—	—	18.4
Sorghum	73	—	—	19.2
Table blends:				
Corn	82	—	—	21.2

VII. FOOD VALUES OF CANDY, SUGAR, & SWEETS

Per Dry Ounce	Total Calories	Grams Protein	Grams Fat	Grams Carbo-hydrates
Cane, maple	71	—	—	18.4
Sugars:				
Beet, cane:				
Brown	106	—	—	27.3
Granulated	109	—	—	28.2
Powdered	109	—	—	28.2
Dextrose:				
Anhydrous	104	—	—	28.2
Crystalized	95	—	—	25.8
Maple	99	—	—	25.5

VIII. FOOD VALUES OF MISCELLANEOUS FOODS

Per Dry Ounce	Total Calories	Grams Protein	Grams Fat	Grams Carbo-hydrates
Bouillon cubes or powder	34	5.7	.9	1.4
Carob flour	51	1.3	.4	22.9
Chewing gum (see candy, sugars, & sweets table)				
Chili con carne (canned, dried at home):				
With beans	105	7.4	3.0	12.1
Without beans	127	9.8	7.0	5.5
Cream substitutes (see milk & milk products table)				
Gelatin	95	24.5	—	—
Malt	104	3.7	.3	21.9
Mustard, prepared, brown	100	6.5	6.9	5.8
yellow	89	5.6	5.3	7.6
Soups, commercial, dry:				
Beef noodle	110	3.9	2.1	18.5
Chicken noodle	109	4.1	2.8	16.4
Chicken rice	100	2.6	1.9	17.8
Onion	99	3.9	3.0	15.3
Pea	103	6.4	1.2	17.4
Tomato vegetable, noodles	99	2.5	2.3	17.7

IX. FOOD VALUES OF ALCOHOLIC BEVERAGES*

	Total Calories	Grams Protein	Grams Fat	Grams Carbo- hydrates
Alcohol:				
80 proof	66	—	—	—
86 proof	70	—	—	—
90 proof	75	—	—	—
100 proof	84	—	—	—
151 proof	134	—	—	—

* *The calories in alcoholic beverages come from ethanol and do not contain protein, fat or carbohydrates. This is the only food with this property.*

X. FOOD VALUES OF SOME STANDARD GROCERY ITEMS

These figures are as given by the manufacturers. It's worth noting that many manufacturers do not give the food value of a product on the package. In these cases, it is reasonably accurate to figure the food value of the main ingredient (such as flour, starch, rice, or potatoes) of the package and deduct 5 to 10 percent if the package includes, or is, a sauce mix.

I

Per Dry Ounce	Total Calories	Grams Protein	Grams Fat	Grams Carbo- hydrates
Dry breads & Mixes:				
Aunt Jemima—regular pancake mix	90	1.6	—	18.7
Hungry Jack Buttermilk pancake mix	118	2.9	1.8	22.5
Crisp Rye bread	111	3.7	—	24.0
Melba toast	112	7.0	—	21.0
Rye Krisp	117	2.3	2.3	18.7
Dromedary—Corn bread mix	117	2.1	4.3	19.2
General Foods—Stove Top Dressing	110	4.0	2.0	19.0

The above is close to the food values of all dried stuffing mixes. General Foods is the only manufacturer that—in my area—includes this information on the package.

II

Per Dry Ounce	Total Calories	Grams Protein	Grams Fat	Grams Carbohydrates
Food Bars & Sticks—toaster varieties:				
Toast 'em—various	109	1.1	2.9	19.4
Pop Tarts—various	115	2.2	3.3	19.1
Nabisco Toastettes—various	117	1.2	3.1	21.5
Nontoaster regular varieties:				
Carnation Breakfast Bar— various	143	4.1	6.8	14.3
Crunchola—various	151	4.7	8.5	14.1
General Mills High Protein Breakfast squares	127	4.0	5.7	15.0
Natural Valley Granola Bar—various	132	2.4	6.0	18.0
Pillsbury Food Sticks	129	2.9	4.3	19.3
Nontoaster *diet* varieties:				
Pillsbury Figurines	147	5.9	8.5	11.2
Sego Bars	145	5.8	7.9	12.6
Instant Breakfasts:				
Carnation Instant Breakfast— various	103	5.6	.8	18.3
Foremost Instant Breakfast— various	107	6.6	.8	18.9
Slenderway—various	108	4.9	1.0	20.0
Maypo—30 second	110	4.0	2.0	20.0
Quaker Instant Oatmeal— various	112	3.2	1.6	20.8
Main dishes:				
Pasta & potato based:				
General Mills—Hamburger Helper:				
Pasta base	97	2.6	.6	20.6
Potato base	114	2.1	2.1	21.4

Per Dry Ounce	Total Calories	Grams Protein	Grams Fat	Grams Carbo-hydrates
Golden Grain Macaroni & Cheese:				
Regular	111	3.9	.6	21.1
Stir & Serve	111	3.9	.6	21.1
Golden Grain Noodle-Roni—				
Parmissano	108	4.2	1.7	19.2
Kraft:				
Macaroni & Cheese	105	4.4	1.1	17.7
Noodle with chicken dinner	103	4.6	2.3	16.6
Tangy style spaghetti dinner	98	4.5	1.0	18.5
Town House—macaroni & cheese	104	3.7	.4	21.1
Rice base:				
Instant rice—various	94	1.7	—	21.4
Minute Rice Mix—various	103	2.6	—	21.4
MJB Brown & wild rice mix	110	2.0	2.0	21.0
Rice-a-roni—various	100	1.9	.6	20.6
Instant puddings & Pie mixes:*				
Chocolate fudge & plain chocolate	98	.9	.9	24.9
Coconut cream	117	3.2	—	23.5
Others (butterscotch, lemon, French vanilla, banana, banana cream, pistachio)	107	—	—	25.6

The above figures are all for JELLO brand—others should be similar. JELLO is the only manufacturer available in my area that puts the food values on the package!

XI. FOOD VALUES OF SOME COMMONLY USED COMMERCIAL TRAIL FOODS
(BY THE DRY OUNCE)

Here are the food values, by the dry ounce, and brand name of 102 commercially packaged and processed trail foods. With the exception of SEIDEL TRAIL PACKETS, all of the figures were adapted from those compiled by Dr. William W. Fogerty, M.D., President of Indiana Camp Supply, Inc.

Dr. Fogerty analyzed all the items carried and sold by Indiana Camp Supply; their catalog lists the food values—by the serving—of over 900 items, processed and packaged by MOUNTAIN HOUSE, TEA KETTLE, RICH MOOR, DRI-LITE, WILSON, CHUCK WAGON, EARTH WONDER, and NATURAL FOOD BACKPACK DINNERS (see page 185).

The figures on SEIDEL TRAIL PACKETS were supplied by SEIDEL, and adapted to dry ounce figures.

As these figures are for finished products, the recipe in use at any one time can vary slightly in food value from those given here.

When purchasing this type of item, the cost versus food value should be considered. Occasionally, a package "for two" will vary in weight per serving from a package "for four."

Per Dry Ounce	Total Calories	Grams Protein	Grams Fat	Grams Carbo-hydrates
Beef stew:				
Chuck Wagon	105	5.1	2.2	16.3
Dri-Lite	102	5.5	2.5	13.5
Mountain House	123	9.4	4.1	12.1
Seidel	107	5.9	2.2	14.4
Vegetable stews with beef:				
Chuck Wagon	105	5.0	2.3	16.4
Mountain House—regular	123	7.1	4.1	14.7
compressed	123	6.8	4.2	14.7
Rich Moor—specialty	105	5.0	2.3	16.5
No Cook	102	5.9	2.7	13.9
Seidel—veg-rice-beef	102	5.1	2.5	14.9
Beef Almondine:				
Teakettle	127	10.0	4.6	11.3
Stroganoff with beef:				
Chuck Wagon	119	5.8	3.7	18.2
Dri-Lite	119	5.8	3.8	15.7
Mountain House	137	5.6	6.7	13.3
Rich Moor—regular	120	5.8	3.8	15.7
instant	116	5.6	3.8	15.7
Seidel	100	5.7	3.6	11.1

Per Dry Ounce	Total Calories	Grams Protein	Grams Fat	Grams Carbo-hydrates
Chili, Beef & Noodle entrees with various names:				
Chuck Wagon—Macaroni— Chuck Wagon Style	102	10.8	—	15.4
Dri-Lite—Chili Mac with beef	95	6.3	1.9	13.4
Mountain House—Chili mac with beef	123	6.8	3.7	15.3
Rich Moor:				
Chili mac with beef	107	5.6	1.7	17.4
Chili Noodle Dinner	102	10.7	—	15.2
Chili & Beans:				
Mountain House—regular	120	12.4	4.0	8.7
compressed	120	12.4	4.0	8.7
Chicken stew:				
Chuck Wagon	111	10.2	2.6	11.5
Mountain House—regular	121	8.7	4.4	11.7
compressed	120	8.8	4.4	11.7
Rich Moor	111	10.1	2.7	11.7
Chicken & Rice (various names):				
Chuck Wagon—Rice & Chicken	105	4.7	1.5	18.1
Mountain House:				
Rice & chicken—regular	126	3.8	4.2	18.3
compressed	126	3.6	4.0	18.2
Chicken Pilaf	129	4.6	4.6	16.8
Rich Moor—Chicken rice dinner	106	5.2	1.9	16.7
Savory chicken & rice	105	5.0	1.3	18.2
Tea Kettle—Chicken with rice	120	7.1	3.6	15.0
Chicken ala King:				
Chuck Wagon	113	7.3	4.4	11.6
Rich Moor	118	5.9	2.2	18.6
Seidel	134	8.5	5.0	13.5
Other chicken dishes (also see Grocery items):				
Chuck Wagon—Good 'n hearty	108	6.9	2.9	13.5

Per Dry Ounce	Total Calories	Grams Protein	Grams Fat	Grams Carbohydrates
Dri-Lite—creamed with noodles	101	6.3	1.3	15.7
and dumplings	103	6.4	1.4	16.0
Mountain House—noodles				
& chicken	126	5.0	5.0	15.5
Seidel—chicken noodle dinner	103	6.5	1.4	16.0
Spaghetti Dishes (also see				
Grocery items):				
Chuck Wagon—with				
tomato sauce	102	5.3	.8	17.9
Dri-Lite—and sauce	106	5.8	.9	18.8
with sauce & meatballs	110	4.9	2.2	17.8
Mountain House—meat				
& sauce	110	4.7	2.4	18.2
Rich Moor—with Italian sauce	102	5.5	.9	17.8
reg. instant	102	5.4	.7	17.8
and meatballs	110	4.8	2.1	18.1
Seidel—spaghetti-beef dinner	96	5.7	.8	16.0
Macaroni & cheese (also see				
Grocery items):				
Chuck Wagon	108	4.4	2.4	16.8
Dri-Lite	108	4.4	2.4	17.2
Mountain House	108	4.4	2.7	16.9
Rich Moor	110	4.7	2.5	16.9
Seidel	108	4.7	2.0	18.0
Tuna dishes:				
Rich Moor—tuna noodle				
casserole	103	7.8	2.4	14.5
Tea Kettle—ala Neptune	125	9.2	3.8	12.0
Turkey Dishes:				
Chuck Wagon—Good 'n hearty	106	6.9	2.9	13.1
Rich Moor—supreme	106	6.9	2.8	13.2
No cook supreme	107	7.0	2.8	13.2
Tea Kettle—Tetrazzini	119	8.5	4.3	11.5
Shrimp Creole:				
Mountain House—regular	121	5.3	3.7	16.3
compressed	128	5.2	3.8	16.2

XI. FOOD VALUES OF SOME COMMONLY USED
COMMERCIAL TRAIL FOODS (Continued)

Per Dry Ounce	Total Calories	Grams Protein	Grams Fat	Grams Carbo-hydrates
Natural Foods:				
Earth Wonder Brand:				
Fruit & nut rice	109	3.3	4.7	13.3
Lentil & whole wheat soup	100	5.1	.3	20.0
Millet stew	99	2.5	.6	22.5
Mushroom & wheat pilaf	66	2.0	.2	14.1
Spanish rice	96	2.0	1.0	19.5
Split pea & barley soup	99	5.1	.4	19.8
Whole wheat salad	103	3.1	—	22.3
Tuna Salad:				
Mountain House	148	10.2	8.7	8.0
Rich Moor	117	23.0	1.0	4.0
Chicken Salad:				
Mountain House	129	9.5	5.8	9.5
Rich Moor	142	12.0	9.3	2.6
Ham Salad:				
Rich Moor	179	13.3	12.0	2.6
Desserts—listed by brand names:				
Chuck Wagon:				
Butterscotch pudding	100	2.9	—	22.5
Chocolate pudding	100	2.9	—	22.5
Fruit Delight	118	—	1.0	27.0
Dri-Lite:				
Butterscotch pudding	105	2.7	.5	26.0
Cheesecake	102	2.3	.8	21.3
Chocolate cream pie	112	2.3	.8	24.0
Chocolate pudding	103	3.2	.5	21.3
Fruit salad	115	—	.7	27.3
Sierra salad	118	—	1.0	27.0
Vanilla pudding	100	2.7	—	22.7
Mountain House:				
Banana cream pudding	104	3.2	—	21.6
Butterscotch pudding	105	2.4	—	23.9
Chocolate ice cream	118	2.8	2.7	21.2
Chocolate pudding	103	3.2	.8	21.6
Strawberry ice cream	129	2.4	4.8	19.2

Per Dry Ounce	Total Calories	Grams Protein	Grams Fat	Grams Carbo-hydrates
Vanilla ice cream	139	2.4	6.8	18.0
Rich Moor:				
Banana cream pudding	104	3.5	—	21.6
Blueberry cobbler	119	.4	2.3	24.0
Butterscotch pudding	104	3.4	.3	21.9
Cherry pie	109	1.1	.7	24.5
Chocolate fudge brownie mix	137	2.0	9.0	14.3
Chocolate pudding	103	3.6	.7	21.6
Lemon pie	109	1.2	.8	24.6
Neapolitan ice cream	123	2.9	4.3	18.6
Pineapple cheese cake	100	2.4	.7	22.3
Raspberry cobbler	107	1.1	.7	24.2

APPENDIX

TEST
REPORT
ON
LIGHT-PACK
STOVES

TESTING NOTE

In the final preparation of this book, I spent 4 weeks testing twenty different models of light-pack stoves. Over 450 individual tests were run using from 1 to 4 units of each model. Our son, Daniel, was my constant companion in this venture.

In talking over the idea of testing light-pack stoves with a number of friends, the consensus was that it would be a worthwhile effort to test for what the average person could expect from the unit, rather than what an expert, working in a controlled environment, could accomplish.

As a result, the tests were run on a covered outdoor patio where there was often a light breeze. I assumed that the user would give the units some wind protection, nothing extreme, but some modest effort—as I did during the tests.

Enough tests were run—averaging a little over twenty per unit—to attain what an engineer friend felt was testing validity. The charts show average times to boil and ranges of times to boil. Anyone should be able to work within the ranges and usually close to the averages on mild days in the field.

When reading the data on the white gasoline and kerosene pump units, it should be noted that at no time did I overpump any unit. Keeping to the basic premise, I pumped what seemed a reasonable number of times, following the instructions given with the stove. It's quite possible to pump one of these units to higher pressures and faster times, but it is not something that would likely be done in the field by an average user.

Before beginning the stoves tests, I tested pot size in relation to efficiency. I used 7-inch, 3-quart, lidded pots in the stove tests because the pot tests showed the 7 inch was 15 percent more efficient than a 6-inch pot and 33 percent more efficient than a 5-inch pot. (As these tests results are based on 7-inch pots—if you use a 6-inch pot, the time to boil should be around 15 percent longer.) With an 8-inch pot, the heat reflected back to the stove increased to a point that didn't seem consistent with safety.

I drilled ½-inch holes in each lid for the thermometer and used standard procedures and equipment. I weighed the water (32 ounces = 1 quart), and used laboratory thermometers and stop watches.

In the "time to boil a quart of water" tests, we began with a water temperature of 70 to 72°F. To bring the water to boil (212°), the stoves had to raise the temperature 140 to 142°. Air temperature ranged from 68 to 75°.

These tests offer a basis for normal-use comparisons among stove types.

On the chart I give, average BTUHs transferred *into* the water. A BTU (British Thermal Unit) is the amount of heat necessary to increase the temperature of 1 pound of water 1°F. A BTUH is the number of BTUs transferred into the water in 1 hour.

A general rule of "fuel-to-carry" is: if melting snow for water, carry 1 cup of fuel per person per day; if water is available, carry half of that. If you become adept at using the OMB (One Minute Boil) cooking method, the fuel necessary to cook will be reduced, but not the fuel to melt the snow.

BOILING TIMES

The standard method of comparison of these units is the time it takes them to bring 1 quart of water to a boil. In this regard, here are some spinoffs worth noting:

1. If a unit takes 5 minutes to bring 1 quart to a boil, the same unit, under the same conditions, will take 10 minutes to bring 2 quarts to a boil and only 2½ minutes to bring ½ quart (1 pint) to a boil.

2. For practical purposes, a quart of water weighs 32 ounces.

   If cooking 5 ounces of dried food in 27 ounces of water, the total is still 32 ounces and the "boil" figures in the chart are still relatively reliable—even though there may be a slight deviation owing to the bulk or type of dried food.

3. In advertising times to bring water to a boil, there is no industry-wide standard starting temperature. For example, some manufacturers start with 70° water (70 to 212°), and others start with 74, 68, and in one notable case, 45°.

   a. Manufacturers, distributors, and importers publish boiling times of their units in sales literature. These are usually determined under optimum conditions—conditions that don't occur outdoors.

   b. The most reliable factor to consider is the number of degrees of increase in temperature per minute for a quart of water. This is a simple way of saying BTUs (British Thermal Units) transferred into the water.

VAPORIZED BUTANE UNITS
(LISTED ALPHABETICALLY)

ALP 7000 (CARTRIDGE: PRIMUS OR BERNZOMATIC)

This excellent unit is an English design by Allan Baxter of Allanter Instruments, Ltd. They are distributed by Rich-Moor in this country.

The cartridge is at the end of a 15-inch rubber tube. This allows some cold-weather use because the cartridge can be kept warm in a bag or by hand. It is also an excellent safety measure because the cartridge is kept away from the heat of the burner. Thus, if you use a shroud, you can drape the shroud as low as you like without draping it over the cartridge.

When packed, it is the smallest of all units tested—only 3½ by 1½ inches.

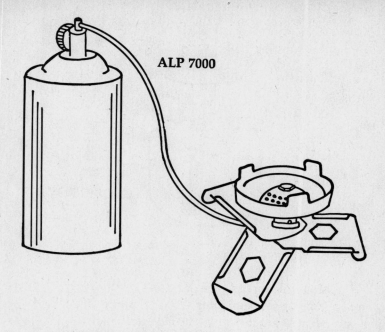

ALP 7000

As the unit uses the Primus cartridge, it allows you to use the cartridge for the stove and for the Primus 2220 Camp Light. The 2220 weighs 10 ounces and gives an excellent, soft light. The cartridge can be easily transferred from one unit to the other (also see Primus Ranger, below).

While I did not test it, there is also a one cartridge, two-burner model of this stove. With this model, you can have a lantern (also Rich-Moor) burning on one burner and at the same time use the other burner for cooking. This two-burner unit weighs 17 ounces without the cartridge and sits up on four rather long legs, and it can be unstable on some surfaces.

GAZ GLOBETROTTER (CARTRIDGE: GAZ GT)

The unit has two small pots which hold slightly over a pint apiece. These nest together to form a 5½ by 4¼-inch carrying case for the stove and cartridge.

159

**GAZ
GLOBETROTTER**

Using these pots, the unit is very slow in heating water, averaging 9:28 minutes to boil 1 quart (actually 4:44 per pint because a quart won't fit into the pot).

When using the standard pots of 7-inch base diameter, the Globetrotter achieved a slightly quicker, although still slow, quart-boil (8:50 minutes, average).

Although the unit's pint pots allow keeping foods separate, a single quart-sized pot with a lid would have allowed greater heating efficiency and greater use on the trail at no increase in weight.

PRIMUS RANGER (CARTRIDGE: PRIMUS OR BERNZOMATIC)

The unit is somewhat difficult to stabilize without an absolutely flat surface.

It produces good boil times averaging 5:43 minutes per quart-boil, and it has excellent simmering capacity.

The price of these attributes is greater weight. It was the heaviest of the butane stoves tested by 5½ to 9 ounces.

Its cartridge also fits the Primus 2220 Camp Light.

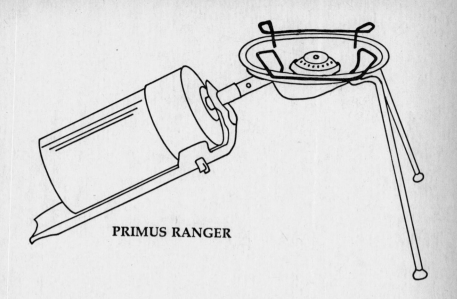

PRIMUS RANGER

PROLITE (CARTRIDGE: PROLIGHT OR SCRIPTO)

The unit uses the same, small butane cartridges that are used to refill butane cigarette lighters, and they are available in most drug and grocery stores. The cartridge is attached at the end of a 31-inch clear plastic tube that also has a 3-inch section of metal tubing between it and the burner stem which lowers the heat transfer to the plastic tube.

This is an excellent safety factor that allows close shrouding of the burner and pot.

Using the small cartridges (net weight 2.35 ounces), the cost per quart-boil was high, running nearly 20 cents per quart. The cost can be cut to around 11 cents a quart by using the larger, 5-ounce cartridges.

In the tests, there was an occasional advantage to placing the cartridge below the level of the stove itself. This was especially true with a new, full cartridge, or one that had been pressurized by sloshing around. In these cases, liquid butane fed to the burner and caused flaring.

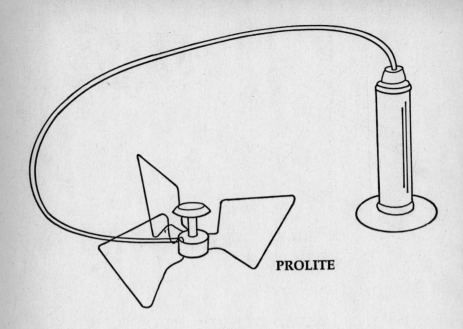

PROLITE

This unit's burner is so exposed to wind that it requires a windscreen, or a heat shroud for optimum operation, even in fair weather.

LIQUID BUTANE STOVES

The following two units operate on the liquid feed principle and do not depend on internal pressure to force fuel from the cartridge into the stove. This assures a good fuel supply to the stove, which in turn allows these two units to operate efficiently in colder weather than the vaporized butane units above. Even so, all Butane freezes solid at 15°F.

E.F.I. MINI STOVE (CARTRIDGE: OPTIMUS, E.F.I., GERRY)

This unit is also sold under the brand names Universal, Gerry, Medalist, and you may run across an older version with a Browning label. When packed for carrying, it breaks

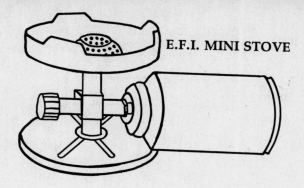

down into a rather small and compact 4½ by 2 inches; it's small enough to carry in a pocket.

The cartridge is horizontally attached to the burner stem. It is a good idea to wet the nipple on the burner stem before attaching the cartridge. This makes attaching the cartridges easier.

With the 7-inch pot, the cartridge picked up a little reflected heat in back-to-back testing. In cold weather, this may be an advantage, but in warm weather and prolonged use, it is advisable to cover the cartridge with aluminum foil to avoid overheating it.

OPTIMUS 731 (CARTRIDGE: OPTIMUS, E.F.I., GERRY)

This is sometimes called the "Mousetrap." It is a flat unit 7 by 4½ by 2 inches when closed. The legs come down, out of the unit, to set it up for use, and this effect is slightly like an old-fashioned mousetrap—hence the nickname.

The fuel is routed past the burner to increase its temperature before going into it. This may account for the slightly better performance than that of the E.F.I.

The metal top gets quite hot, and as the control knob is positioned in a slot in the top, it is difficult to use without touching the hot metal.

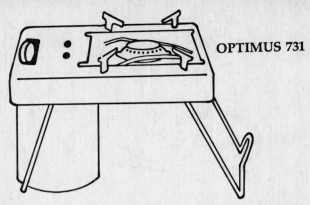

OPTIMUS 731

The 7-inch pot caused stability problems. With a 6-inch pot these disappeared, but the fuel consumed per quart-boil rose.

All figures on the chart are with the 7-inch pot.

WHITE GASOLINE
(SELF-GENERATING UNITS)

OPTIMUS 80 (ALSO CALLED PRIMUS 71L)

The units tested (two new and one old) were all basically Primus 71Ls with an Optimus decal stuck over the Primus. The new and old units were identical.

This is the only self-generating unit still available *without* a built-in cleaning needle. It was also the only self-generating unit tested that would simmer when hot.

Since the burner plate is not tightly fastened to the burner head, it can become detached and lost on a trip. (This is also true of the SVEA 123, the OPTIMUS 8R, and the OPTIMUS 99.) You can remedy this by drilling ¹⁄₁₆-inch holes in one of the burner plate flanges and in the burner head, and fastening them together with a loose metal ring. Or, easier still, be absolutely certain the burner plate is always with you.

Also a slot can be made on the front panel (inside) to hold the cleaning tool.

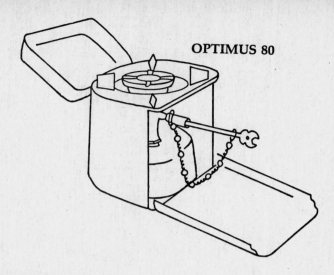

OPTIMUS 88

This is a nesting pot and windscreen (Edelweiss-type) cookset that uses an Optimus (Svea) 123 UR (stripped version) as the heat source.

It is an extremely pleasant, light, and compact unit. However the pots (two included) hold only 3 and 4½ cups of water respectively, when filled to the brim.

The "fry" pan has a 6-inch diameter, and serves best as a lid.

The design is attractive and well made. All Edelweiss designs are slightly inefficient in that they bounce the heat away from the sides of the pot, thereby requiring slightly more fuel (and time) than the heat source normally does.

A fuel-consuming, double boiler effect can be had by putting an inch of water in the smaller pot and mounting the larger over it. This same effect makes the unit well adapted to the OMB (One Minute Boil) method of cooking. The larger pot can be brought to a boil and placed over the smaller pot, while the smaller pot is being heated.

Because of the small size of the pots, it's basically a

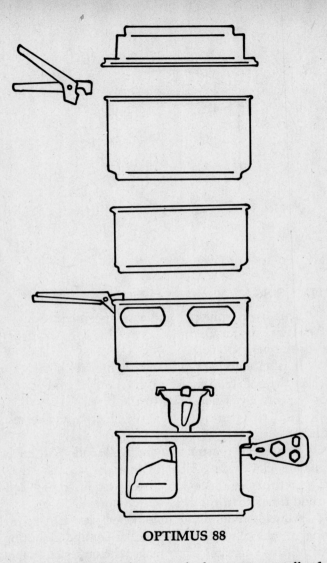

OPTIMUS 88

one-person affair, although it may do for two, especially if you use the OMB technique described above.

Larger versions of the Edelweiss design are available and likely better for two or three people.

OPTIMUS 8R (AND THE OPTIMUS 99)

The OPTIMUS 8R and the 99 have the same stove unit with different cases around them. The 8R has a steel case that is strictly for carrying the stove, although the top might double as a windscreen. The 8R weighs 26 ounces.

The 99 has an aluminum case (the top of which serves as a small pot—3½ cup capacity, filled to the brim) and a small, 2 ounce windscreen. It weighs 23 ounces.

The fuel tanks are mounted beside the burner with only 1½ inches separating them at the closest point. This necessitates a heat shield between the burner and the tank. This shield must be kept from touching the fuel tank and transmitting heat to it, or the unit can overheat.

Tested cold, they were extremely slow to heat water. The quart-to-boil times ranged from 11 to 12 minutes. In a series of three successive boils, the units became warm enough to boil the last quart in a bit over 7 minutes.

The Optimus Minipump (2 ounces) fits the Optimus 80, the 88, the 123, the 8R, and 99. It will increase the pressure in their tanks quite well and speed the time to boil (no figures on the charts include this additional pressure). The pump is awkward to use with all except the 8R and 99 models,

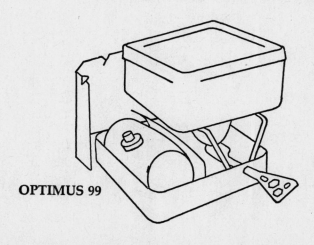

OPTIMUS 99

for which it was apparently designed. When these two units are pumped, they turn in a respectable boiling time of from 5 to 6 minutes for a quart of water.

In my opinion, if you have either and like it, fine. But there are many better buys available. The tanks are very small (2¼ ounces), and the units are quite heavy. Even for a weekend, you have to have a bottle of fuel.

When you add the Minipump and fuel bottle to the weight, it comes to—without fuel—32 ounces for the 8R, and 29 ounces for the 99. And that's a lot of weight for a self-generating unit. Because of the small fuel tank, neither of these units can be considered usable in cold weather.

OPTIMUS (SVEA) 123

This is the unit you see most on the trail. Sales run around 75,000 per year in this country alone. It was the first light-pack stove with a good distribution, and often—10 years or so ago—the only one you would find.

It's a good unit with a good reputation that, despite the somewhat small tank size (it's good for a day or two of cooking for one person), still holds its own in popularity against newer, and sometimes, in my opinion, better designs.

It's rated at 18½ ounces, but 3 ounces are devoted to the aluminum cap (cup) which can be left at home.

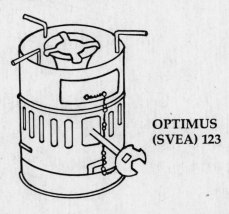

OPTIMUS
(SVEA) 123

PHOEBUS 725

This is the fastest and most fuel-efficient of the self-generating units according to my tests (I worked with three of these). From a cold start, it's 20 to 37 percent faster and from 8 to 27 percent more fuel-efficient than any other self-generating stove.

The tank (7¼ ounces) is large enough for two people on a 2- or 3-day trip, or for one person on a 4- or 5-day trip in mild weather. It's also efficient and hot enough to be the only self-generating unit that is a good cold-weather stove.

Why is the 725 so efficient? The burner is the main answer. It's made of thinner metal than the other self-generating units' burners, and heats up faster. It's also not a "common" plate burner. The main plate has a hole in it that vaporized fuel goes through and a small "target" burner, about ⅛ inch above the plate burner, that the vaporized fuel hits. As it is heated from above and below, the fuel burns very hot. The weight can be cut a couple of ounces by using aluminum pot supports in place of the steel ones.

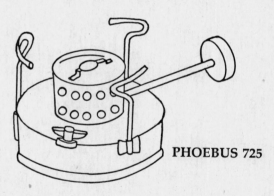

PHOEBUS 725

WHITE GASOLINE STOVES WITH BUILT-IN PUMPS

These are the units that will work in cold weather when others won't. They range from the lightest of all the white gasoline units (the M.S.R. 9A and M.S.R. MF) to the heaviest (the Optimus 111B).

For efficient use, the leather cup located inside the pump should be kept oiled and flexible.

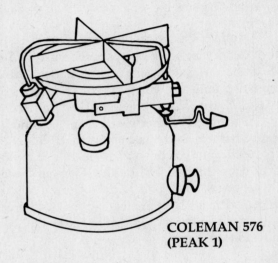

**COLEMAN 576
(PEAK 1)**

COLEMAN 576 (PEAK 1)

This is a new unit designed by Coleman of Canada and modified slightly for sales in the United States. It's efficient and simmers well, the best of the white gasoline units. It's reasonably light for a pump unit (32 ounces) and, under normal conditions, is the only white gasoline unit that does not require priming.

The design is compact and stable. In performance it's the closest thing to a regular stove in the white gasoline units. It's also the lowest priced of the pump units and well within, below in some cases, the price range of the self-generating units. In tank size it's well above the self-generating units (10 ounces), but it's in the lower range of pump units.

The unit is very quiet in operation and with the relatively low price, is a good buy.

M.S.R. 9A (also see M.S.R. MF page 174)

What the buyer receives is a "heat transfer system" that's light, dependable, and extremely efficient. It's the lightest of all the white gasoline units—by a fair to very large margin. In testing and field use, we experienced no problems and no complications.

The weights shown in the accompanying table include the "heat reflector and windscreen," both well designed—and a pint fuel bottle.

As purchased, the unit includes an excellent pump, the burner unit (which has a 6-inch metal tube to attach to the pump, which is carried in the fuel bottle), a heat reflector, a windscreen, a cup to hold the burner unit, and a can lid which helps diffuse the heat when simmering.

For a fuel tank, the unit uses a Sigg (brand name) bottle—either the 1 pint or 1 quart—which must be purchased separately.

M.S.R. 9A
(windscreen—broken line)

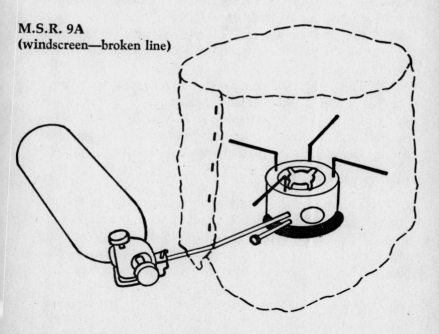

This M.S.R. 9A is an extremely efficient, stable, well-thought-out unit, obviously designed by people who used and tested it afield.

One further point, the unit's operating instructions were the best of all manufacturers.

The only problem might be finding one. Production is only a few thousand units per year. However, you can order direct from M.S.R. whose address is included in the address section.

OPTIMUS 111B

This is similar in design to the Optimus 8R and 99. The steel box that holds the stove itself weighs 30 ounces. The fuel tank and the burner assembly weigh an additional 24 ounces. These can be removed from the box, mounted in various Edelweiss cook sets and carried in the set.

When this is done the fuel tank is outside of the Edelweiss shell, and the high rate of heat transfer from the burner to the tank is cut appreciably. As sold, the unit has a heat shield (similar to the Optimus 8R and 99) which is necessary to protect the fuel tank from the heat of the side-by-side burner assembly.

This heat shield *must* be kept about ½ inch away from the fuel tank to avoid overheating the tank. Even in the first series of testing, the heat shield—on a back-to-back test—bubbled and its plating dissolved on one side. If the shield isn't properly adjusted, the tank can get very hot.

PHOEBUS 625

This is the only unit tested (and available) with a "tulip-style, ported" burner. It's very quiet in operation.

The Phoebus 625 and the 725 (see self-governing units, earlier) have been made as they are, since the late 1950s. They have been available in the United States since 1972.

The 625 is a standard expedition stove. It's been car-

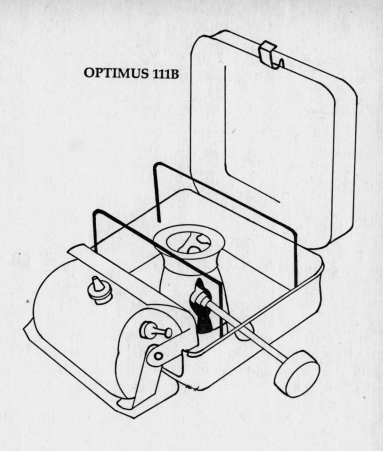

OPTIMUS 111B

ried by Austrian, German, Swiss, and U.S. expeditions in the Andes, the Alps, and the Himalayas as well as McKinley and Northern Canada. It was carried by the American Nanda Devi expedition (1976 Adams Carter and Willi Unsoeld), on the Raidak River descent (1976 Wick Walker), and on McKinley (stranded with Mitch Michaud for 52 days).

It comes in a brightly colored can—which in home use is a storage and display container. In light-pack field use, the can is usually left at home.

The unit itself has a 17-ounce tank and weighs 30

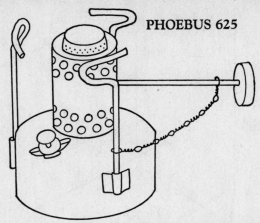

ounces. This can be cut 3 ounces by substituting aluminum pot supports and burner control stem for the steel parts.

It has excellent simmer capability.

KEROSENE STOVES

Kerosene units were once standards. The fuel is available almost anywhere. With the advent of white gasoline and butane they went—temporarily—into limbo. The M.S.R. MF stove is likely to have changed that and may well popularize this fuel again.

M.S.R. MF

The M.S.R. MF (Multifuel) unit is a fine one. Everything good about the M.S.R. 9A (see above) applies to the MF and more.

The unit will burn white gasoline as the M.S.R. 9A (the statistics of the M.S.R. 9A also apply to the M.S.R. MF) and also kerosene, A-50 Jet Fuel, Stoddards Solvent, and Stove Oil.

It's extremely easy to start; as with the M.S.R. 9A a pad (asbestos) is installed under the burner. This absorbs a little fuel released from the tank and onto the pad, which is then lit to prime the stove.

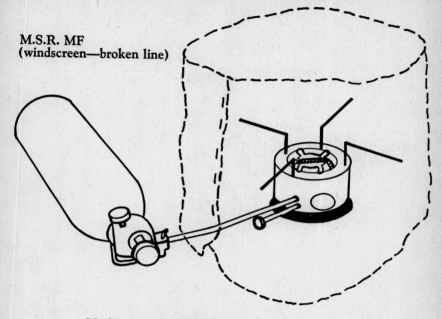

Unfortunately, finding one may prove difficult. As
with the M.S.R. 9A, production figures are low, but the unit
can be purchased from M.S.R. directly (see address section).

OPTIMUS 00L

The unit is attractive. My test model is sitting, well-
polished, as an art object in our living room. Basically the
Optimus 00L is a unit sold for home use, I imagine, mostly in
the Middle East. The Arabic script on it enhances its appearance.

Its weight can be cut 2 to 3 ounces by substituting
aluminum for the steel pot supports.

Stability is worrisome because the unit balances on
three little feet that unfold. The unit has an efficient pump,
and relighting is best done slowly at low pressures: otherwise
the flame takes some time to "quiet down" from a bright-
yellow flame to efficient blue flames.

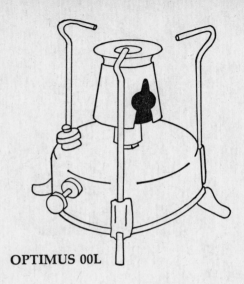

OPTIMUS 00L

Controlling the "simmer" requires using a pressure bleed on the filler cap. Between the pump and the pressure bleed, reasonable simmer is possible.

A heat shroud or windscreen is a must in all but the most clement of weather, for the burner is very exposed to the wind.

ALCOHOL

OPTIMUS 77A

This is the only alcohol unit available. It includes two pots and a "fry pan/lid." It employs a version of the "fondue" pot alcohol burner. It's easy to use and for one or two people is an inexpensive and lightweight "kitchen."

Disadvantages include a high fuel consumption and a build-up of soot on the pots. The instructions recommend covering the burner with the lid to turn it off. The unit I

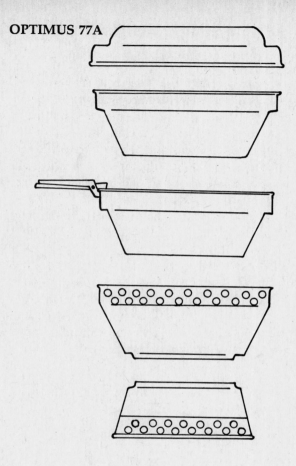

tested was consistently too hot to turn off by this method. When the burner lid was placed over the burner, vaporized alcohol flamed out from all the joints. It was necessary to smother the flame by placing an empty tuna can over it.

There is a simmer ring included with the unit. The efficiency of the ring was still open to doubt after a long series of tests.

Once mastered, the unit was fun and easy to work with and—for short trips—effective for one or two people.

SOLID FUEL

ZIP ZTOVE

The Zip is probably the only solid-fuel stove on the market. It's a small forced-air furnace that will burn any solid fuel such as wood, charcoal, paraffin-impregnated woodwaste, pine cones, and charcoal from old campfires.

Weighing 13½ ounces plus the weight of the "C" battery (1½ ounces) necessary to operate the small fan in the base, it can be the lightest of all the light-pack stoves, provided you don't carry fuel for it.

You can carry a small amount of paraffin-impregnated woodwaste and use portions of it to start a fire of very damp wood scraps.

With the fan turned on, the unit will start a fire very quickly. Within 30 seconds or so a flame will be shooting up in a narrow 1 foot tall column, propelled by the fan. With the fan on, it burns very hot and will bring a quart to boil in from 4 to 4½ minutes. Additional fuel can be slid under the pot, or you can simply lift the pot and drop fuel into the unit.

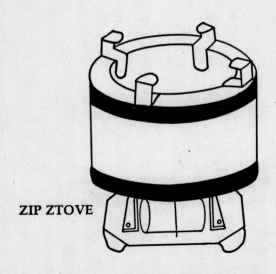

ZIP ZTOVE

If the fan is used throughout the cooking, the battery that energizes the fan will last for only an hour or two of cooking.

Normal usage dictates that the fan be used to start the fire and then be turned off. In this way, the battery will last about a week, and the quart-to-boil times are from 9 to 15 minutes.

It's easy to simmer. Just control the amount of fuel. When finished cooking, I simply let the fuel burn out, as you would any campfire. If using solid fuel that you carry with you, douse it with water so that you can reuse it.

If you are using larger pieces of solid fuel, the unit burns cooler than if you were using smaller pieces. For the hottest fire—break the fuel into small pieces.

It is a very light and useful unit with a rather small production. It can be ordered direct from the manufacturer (see address section).

STERNO AND HEAT TABLETS

Just to keep things "level," I conducted a number of tests on these two heat sources.

A large 7-ounce can of Sterno will bring a quart of water to a boil in 15 to 17 minutes in a coffee-can type stove. The large can will bring up to 5 quarts of water to a boil.

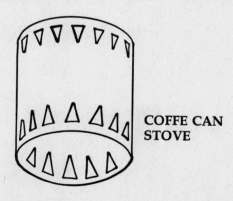

COFFE CAN
STOVE

A small can of Sterno will bring a quart to a boil in 18 to 22 minutes, and will bring, if you're lucky, 2 quarts to a boil, using a coffee-can stove.

There are cases where Sterno is the lightest heat source. If you are out in mild weather for a day or two, and not hurried, it may be a good choice.

A coffee-can stove is made by taking a 1-pound coffee can, cutting the ends off, and making holes (I used a beer can opener) around the base to let fresh air in, and around the top to let hot air out. The pot is set on top.

Heat Tablets were designed to heat military rations, and not to boil water. They also "pop" occasionally and scatter bits of burning material as far as 15 feet. I've been told that this effect may be due to the age of the tablets, but "pops" have occurred with surplus military tablets as well as newly manufactured tablets.

TEST RESULTS   WHITE GASOLINE, KEROSENE, ALCOHOL, & SOLID FUEL UNITS

Unit	Stove weight empty	Fuel tank capacity ounces	Average fuel consumed per quart to boil (ounces)	Approx. quarts to boil per tankful of fuel (4)	Approx. total burning time for tankful	Range of time to boil one quart
			White gasoline (self-generating units)			
OPTIMUS 80	18	4½	.47	6–8	45 min	4:53–8:17
OPTIMUS 88	22 (5)	4	.59	4–5	42 min	7:15–9:00
OPTIMUS 8R	26 (5)	2¼	See accompanying text			7:02–11:46
OPTIMUS 99	23 (5)	2¼	See accompanying text			7:02–11:46
OPTIMUS (SVEA) 123	18½	4	.55	5–6	35 min	5:34–8:08
PHOEBUS 725	22½	7½	.43	11–13	1 hr 7 min	3:50–6:51
		White gasoline (built-in pressure pump units)				
COLEMAN 576 (PEAK 1)	32	10	.55	13–15	1 hr 20 min	3:01–4:49
M.S.R. 9A	18 (1) (5)	12 (1)	.47	25–28 (1)	1½ hr (1)	3:00–3:43
OPTIMUS 111B	54	11¼	.57	14–16	1¼ hr	4:04–4:34
PHOEBUS 625	30	17½	.55	22–24	1 hr 25 min	3:12–4:00
			Kerosene units			
M.S.R. MF	19 (1) (5)	13½ (1)	.47	26–29 (1)	1½ hr (1)	2:24–3:37
OPTIMUS 00L	23	16	.69	16–18	2 hr 10 min	5:10–10:10
			Alcohol unit			
OPTIMUS 77A	24 (5)	2½	.99	2	15–20 min	6:05–8:35
			Solid fuel			
ZIP STOVE	13½	See accompanying text				4:00– ?

TEST RESULTS WHITE GASOLINE, KEROSENE, ALCOHOL, & SOLID FUEL UNITS
(Continued)

Unit	Average time to boil one quart	Range temp. increase per minute	Average temp. increase per minute	Average BTUH into water	Simmer	Cold weather use	Price (3)
		White gasoline (self-generating units)					
OPTIMUS 80	6:40	17–28	21	2520	fair	Maybe (2)	28.00
OPTIMUS 88	8:25	15–19	17	2040	no	Maybe (2)	40.00
OPTIMUS 8R	See accompanying text				no	No	31.00
OPTIMUS 99	See accompanying text				no	No	34.00
OPTIMUS (SVEA) 123	6:55	18–25	21	2520	no	Maybe (2)	29.00
PHOEBUS 725	5:19	21–36	27	3240	no	Yes	27.00
		White gasoline (built-in pressure pump units)					
COLEMAN 576 (PEAK 1)	3:48	29–47	37	4440	good	Yes	27.00
M.S.R. 9A	3:23	37–47	42	5040	fair	Yes	39.00
OPTIMUS 111B	4:21	30–35	33	3960	fair	Yes	58.00
PHOEBUS 625	3:42	32–43	37	4440	good	Yes	37.00
		Kerosene units					
M.S.R. MF	3:08	37–58	45	5400	fair	Yes	41.00
OPTIMUS 00L	7:41	16–27	18	2160	fair	Yes	34.00
		Alcohol unit					
OPTIMUS 77A	7:36	15–23	19	2280	fair	Yes	18.00
		Solid fuel					
ZIP ZTOVE	See accompanying text						16.00

(1) These figures are for the M.S.R. 9A and MF models with a 1-quart fuel container. If you use a 1-quart fuel container, double these figures (see text).

(2) Moderate use in cold weather is possible if the Optimus Mini pump is used.

(3) Prices are manufacturers list prices in 1977.

(4) Figures are based on filling stove's tank ¾ full.

(5) Weights include pots and/or windscreens. For details see accompanying text for each unit.

TEST RESULTS BUTANE UNITS

Unit	Stove weight without cartridge ounces	Cartridge weight empty ounces	Cartridge weight full ounces	Fuel consumed per quart to boil ounces	Approx. quarts to boil per cartridge	Approx. total burning time per cartridge	Range time to boil one quart
		Vaporized butane units					
ALP 7000	6	3.5	10	.44	12–14	1½ hr	6:45–8:00
GAZ GLOBETROTTER	17½ (5)	2.5	5.7	.60	4–5	45 min	8:12–10:10
PRIMUS RANGER	15	3.5	10	.40	14–16	1½ hr	5:15–5:55
PROLITE	7.5	1.3	2.35	.43	4–5	30 min	5:20–6:55
		Liquid butane units					
E.F.I.	7.75	4.25	10.5	.50	10–12	1 hr 20 min	6:01–8:02
OPTIMUS 731	12	4.25	10.5	.45	11–13	1½ hr	5:30–7:23

TEST RESULTS BUTANE UNITS (Continued)

Unit	Average time to boil one quart	Range temp. increase per minute	Average temp. increase per minute	Average BTUH into water	Simmer	Cold weather use	Price (3)
			Vaporized butane units				
ALP 7000	7:20	17–21	19	2280	good	No (see text)	14.95
GAZ GLOBETROTTER	9:28	14–17	15	1800	good	No	19.95
PRIMUS RANGER	5:43	23–27	25	3000	good	No	16.95
PROLITE	6:05	20–26	23	2760	good	No (see text)	8.95
			Liquid butane units				
E.F.I.	6:39	17–23	20	2400	good	No (see text)	19.00
OPTIMUS 731	6:28	19–29	22	2640	good	No (see text)	21.00

ADDRESSES OF SUPPLIERS

DEHYDRATORS
DRI-MOR
C.M.C.
351 West 2450 North
Box 3383
Logan, Utah 84321

ZEPHYR
Zephyr Mfg. Co.
POB 1025
Santa Cruz, Calif. 95061

COMMERCIAL TRAIL FOODS
Indiana Camp Supply, Inc.
POB 344
Pittsboro, Ind. 46167
(317) 547-1134

Siedel's Trail Packets
National Packaged Trail Foods
18607 St. Clair
Cleveland, Ohio 44110

STOVES
ALP 7000
Rich-Moor
P.O. Box 2728
Van Nuys, Calif. 91404

Coleman (Peak 1)
The Coleman Co.
250 N. St. Francis Ave.
Wichita, Kans. 67201

E.F.I.
E. F. Industries
1301 Courtesy Rd.
Louisville, Col. 80027

GAZ
See your retail store

M. S. R.
Mountain Safety Research, Inc.
631 South 96th St.
Seattle, Wash. 98108

Optimus
Optimus-Princess Co.
P.O. Box 3448
Santa Fe Springs, Calif. 90670

Phoebus
Precise Imports
3 Chestnut St.
Suffern, N.Y. 10901

Primus
Primus-Sievert Co.
354 Sackett Point Rd.
North Haven, Conn. 06473

Prolite
Halstead Imports, Inc.
705 Traction Ave.
Los Angeles, Calif. 90013

Zip Ztove
Z. Z. Corp.
10806 Kaylor St.
Los Alamitos, Calif. 90720

INDEX

188

194

Catalog

If you are interested in a list of fine Paperback
books, covering a wide range of subjects
and interests, send your name and address,
requesting your free catalog, to:

McGraw-Hill Paperbacks
1221 Avenue of Americas
New York, N.Y. 10020